FIRE

Arsenal Pulp Press | Vancouver

FIRE

A QUEER FILM CLASSIC

Shohini Ghosh

ARSENAL PULP PRESS
211 East Georgia Street, Suite 101
Vancouver, BC V6A 1Z6 Canada
arsenalpulp.com

Efforts have been made to locate copyright holders of source material wherever possible. The publisher welcomes hearing from any copyright holders of material used
in this book who have not been contacted.

Queer Film Classics series editors: Matthew Hays and Thomas Waugh

Cover and text design by Shyla Seller
Edited for the press by Susan Safyan
All film stills (except where indicated) © Zeitgeist Films
Filmography compiled by Samuel Burd
Author photograph by Sohail Akbar

Mixed Sources

Cert no. SW-COC-001271
© 1996 FSC

FSC

Printed and bound in Canada

CANADIAN CATALOGUING IN PUBLICATION DATA

Ghosh, Shohini, 1961-
        Fire / Shohini Ghosh.

(A queer film classic)
Includes bibliographical references and index.
Issued also in electronic format.
ISBN 978-1-55152-363-7

        1. Fire (Motion picture). 2. Mehta, Deepa—Criticism and
interpretation. I. Title. II. Series: Queer film classics

PN1997.F465G56 2010   791.43'72   C2010-905894-1

To
Ma and Baba
For giving me life and the freedom to be who I am

and
Chungee
My beautiful dog and perfect companion

CONTENTS

ACKNOWLEDGMENTS

While writing is a lonely activity, no scholarship is possible without an intellectual community and therefore my debts are many. My greatest debt is to the Sexuality and Rights Institute (CREA & TARSHI) for providing an intellectually stimulating environment for provocative debates. I am especially grateful to Geetanjali Misra, Radhika Chandiramani, Carole Vance, and Ali Miller for being wonderful friends and fearless thinkers. I am grateful to Ranjani Mazumdar and Sabeena Gadihoke whose friendship, support, and criticism I take for granted and whose work inspires my own. Their legitimate doubts about my finishing this book in two months pushed me to race against the deadline. Over two decades, I have been sustained by the friendship and intelligence of Ruth Vanita, Sara Hossain, Joya Chatterjee, Ratna Kapur, Saleem Kidwai, Syeda Syedain Hameed, Geeta Patel, Uma Chakravarty, and Tanika Sarkar. Their excellent work in their respective disciplines has no doubt shaped my arguments. I am grateful to the generosity of the McArthur-Globalization Fellowship (2001) at the University of Chicago for giving me time and space to work through many of the ideas in this book. I am especially grateful to Arjun Appadurai, Carol Breckenridge, Dipesh Chakrabarty, and Jacqueline Bhaba for making my stay both comfortable and intellectually stimulating.

I am deeply indebted to Shabana Azmi and Nandita Das for sharing their experiences with me. In different ways, both are important in my life, so I hope this book can be a tribute to their strength and spirit. Very special thanks to Nandita for our long years of friendship and for trusting me with her personal archives on *Fire*. I also want to thank Aradhana Seth and Payal Randhawa for generously sharing their experiences of working on the film. For helping with the project in many ways, I am grateful to Sabina Kidwai, Sohail Akbar, Loveleen Tandan, Shikha Jhingan, Sealing Cheng, Seema Alavi, Brinda Bose and the James Beveridge Media Resource Centre at Jamia Millia Islamia.

This volume wouldn't exist without the encouragement of Tom Waugh and Matthew Hays. Tom's body of work has been a source of personal inspiration for years. I cannot thank Tom and Samuel Burd enough for becoming long-distance research associates and helping me access material from Canada. At Arsenal Pulp Press, I am grateful to Brian Lam, Shyla Seller, and Susan Safyan for their excellent support.

My deep gratitude to Rituparno Ghosh—my favourite film and "adda" mate—for the richness he brings to my life. I am grateful to Sharmila Tagore for our shared cinephilia, Margot Francis for our strong transatlantic bond, and Arundhati Roy for her imagination and deep insights. My special thanks to Momin Jaan for all that we share in life and films. I am deeply indebted to my sister Shahana Bose and my brother-in-law D.K. Bose who left us too early but never really did. The three of us have grown up with films—a world as real for us as any other. Thanks to Rukmini, Tia, and Manish for suffering neglect during the writing of the book and to Sabita and Santosh Sen for their boundless faith and good wishes. Many thanks to Lata for bringing order to the chaos I call my home and to my four beautiful cats—two gone but still here—Moju, Dawood, Burfi, and Xerox.

SYNOPSIS

New Delhi, mid-1990s. Sita joins the extended Kapur family after an arranged marriage to the younger brother, Jatin, who runs a video rental store. Radha, married to Jatin's elder brother Ashok, runs the household including the family's take-out business. The family also includes Biji, Ashok and Jatin's aging mother who has been left mute and paralyzed by a severe stroke. Biji,[1] as everyone calls her, is looked after by Radha and Mundu, the overworked, live-in male servant. Neither Jatin nor Ashok are particularly interested in their wives. Since Radha has not been able to bear him any children, Ashok embraces celibacy so as not to indulge in sex outside of procreation. He believes that "desire is the root of all evil" and strives to transcend all temptation under the guidance of his spiritual guru in whose ashram he prefers to spend his time and money. Jatin is devoted to Julie, his long-time Indian-Chinese girlfriend who has refused to marry him as she does not want to live in a joint family and become a "baby-making machine." Jatin cannot stop seeing Julie and so makes no effort to offer Sita either friendship or affection.

Sita starts helping Radha with the family business and

1. Biji (Mother) is usually used to refer to the maternal head of the family. Therefore, grandchildren or other members of the extended family often use the term as both an affectionate and respectful form of address.

finds herself increasingly drawn to her sister-in-law's quiet beauty and tenderness. Radha is also attracted to the irreverent and passionate Sita who, unlike her, is not afraid of questioning tradition and custom. The women become increasingly close and soon fall in love. Domestic work no longer seems like drudgery, as the gendered regimen of everyday life provides the lovers space and opportunity to nurture their relationship. They visit the shrine of the Sufi mystic Hazrat Nizamuddin Auliya (1238–1325) and pray for a life together. Despite Biji and Mundu's mounting suspicions and growing discomfiture, they manage to keep their relationship undetected.

One day, Radha discovers Mundu masturbating to a porn video in the living room as Biji looks on in horror and helplessness. An outraged Radha slaps Mundu and threatens to throw him out. Mundu feels humiliated and threatens to divulge Radha's relationship with Sita. Unnerved by his temerity, Radha demands that Mundu be sacked, but Ashok forgives his youthful folly and gives him another chance. The household returns to its regular routine, but Mundu now starts to act cocky with Radha. One evening, he spies on the two women through the keyhole and overhears Sita say that they should leave their marriages and run away. Mundu immediately goes to the ashram and tells Ashok.

Ashok rushes home, but before confronting the lovers, he sacks Mundu. Through the crack in the door, Ashok watches Radha make love to Sita and barges into the room. As the family scandal begins to erupt, it becomes urgent for the women to leave. Sita leaves the house first and promises to wait for Radha at the Nizamuddin Shrine. Radha stays back to have a last conversation with Ashok. Meanwhile, the specter of the two women making love haunts Ashok until he is wracked by rage and arousal. During her final confrontation with Ashok, Radha's sari accidentally catches fire on the kitchen stove. As she struggles to put out the flames, Ashok carries Biji away, leaving Radha to her fate.

On this rainy night, Sita waits at the Sufi shrine. Radha finally arrives, bruised and scorched, but having somehow made her way out alive. The ordeal by fire over, Radha and Sita are reunited.

CREDITS

Fire
1996
India
English (original) Hindi (dubbed)
107 min., 58 seconds, Color, 1.85 : 1, Ultra-Stereo
MPAA rating; PG-13 /(CBFC Certificate: A)
Trial by *Fire* Films, Guild Film Distribution
Director: Deepa Mehta
Executive Producers: Suresh Bhalla, David Hamilton
Producers: Bobby Bedi, Deepa Mehta
Writer: Deepa Mehta

Principal Cast
Shabana Azmi: Radha
Nandita Das: Sita
Kulbhushan Kharbanda: Ashok
Jaaved Jaaferi: Jatin
Ranjit Chowdhry: Mundu
Kushal Rekhi: Biji
Alice Poon: Julie
Ram Gopal Bajaj: Swamiji

Crew
Cinematography: Giles Nuttgens
Editor: Barry Farrell
Production Designer: Aradhana Seth
Art Direction: Sunil Chabra
Costume Design: Neelam Mansingh Chowdhury, Anju
  Rekhi
Music: A.R. Rahman

Filmed in Delhi, India.
Premiered: September 6, 1996 at the Toronto International
  Film Festival; October 2 at the New York Film Festival.
Awards: Barcelona International Women's Film
  Festival, Los Angeles Outfest, Mannheim-Heidelberg
  International Film Festival, Vancouver International
  Film Festival, Verona Love Screens Film Festival.

INTRODUCTION

When *Fire* was first released in India, I wrote a review that lauded the film for daring to "rework the heterosexist myth that women in love must remain invisible on screen" and predicted that for this very reason its place in the history of Indian cinema was assured. However, my largely favorable review included a damning paragraph. I wrote:

> It is unlikely that *Fire* will go down in cinematic history as a great film. It is a film that is significant more for its content than its treatment. The story, characters and plot are neither rich nor textured. The sights and sounds of Lajpat Nagar lack depth and nuances. The mimetic quality of realism that the film adopts works to its detriment. Even the tropes of Hindu cultural practices remain direct and uncomplicated. Perhaps, the tritest mythical reference is the very literal *agni pariksha* with its oft–repeated resonance of *sati* and dowry murders.[2] With the exception of the performances of its protagonists, the film is unlikely to improve on second viewing. (Ghosh 1999c)

But as it turned out, *Fire* was not easy to dismiss. Once it

---

2. *Agni pariksha* is trial by fire.

FIGURE 1. The photographs used for the posters of *Fire* were shot by well known photographer Atul Kasbekar. (Courtesy: Nandita Das)

arrived, it refused to leave even after the film was taken out of theaters. It acquired a hectic social life and circulated in the public imagination, inspiring admirers and haunting detractors. Every time I wrote about queerness and cinema in India, I found it hard not to connect it to some insight I had gained from the experience of seeing and discussing *Fire*. Yet the debates prised open by this film were not to do with issues of sexuality alone. This volume, therefore, is an attempt to revisit the film in light of the innumerable insights I have gained in the last twelve years. In her introduction to her autobiography *Pentimento*, Lillian Hellman explains that when old paint on canvas ages, it reveals the original lines the painter had painted. For her memoir, she appropriates the traditional term for this phenomenon, called "pentimento" because the painter repented. When the old conception is replaced by a later choice, it is a way of seeing and then seeing again. I see the writing of this volume as my pentimento—an attempt to understand what I saw then and what I see now.

Indo-Canadian filmmaker Deepa Mehta's *Fire* is a love story set in a middle-class Hindu household in Delhi. Starring India's noted actress Shabana Azmi and then debutante actress Nandita Das, the film is about two sisters-in-law who fall in love. The film premiered in 1996, traveled the international circuit for about two years, and was finally released in India in November 1998. As the distributors got ready to release the English (original) and Hindi (dubbed) versions, posters and billboards advertising the film appeared all over the city. It was new and exciting to see two women inhabit the space that had conventionally belonged to heterosexual couples. None of the posters made explicit that the women were lovers, but their intimate proximity was poised precariously (and pleasurably) on the tantalizing borderline of friendship and eroticism. For the first time in the world's largest film producing country, lesbian love became visible in the public sphere. To everyone's surprise (pleasant or otherwise), the Indian Central Board of Film Certification (CBFC) passed the film without cuts but insisted on a seemingly slight but significant modification. They asked that in the Hindi version, the name of the younger sister-in-law (played by Nandita Das) should be changed from Sita to Nita. This change was clearly recommended as a precautionary measure so as not to offend the Hindu Right, as the two women—Radha and Sita—had been named after two revered female goddesses of the Hindu pantheon. Sita, the dutiful, self-effacing wife of Ram, the principal protagonist of the Hindu epic *Ramayana*, is considered by the Hindu Right to be the epitome of womanhood.[3] A few weeks after *Fire* was released, the Hindu Right unleashed their fury

---

3. According to Hindu mythology, Radha is the lover of the god Krishna, and in some versions, she is a married woman who is older than her youthful lover. The passionate love of Radha and Krishna was immortalized in the twelfth-century dramatic lyrical poem *Gita Govinda* composed by Jaiyadeva. The frank eroticism of the poetry

upon the film.[4] Rampaging mobs vandalized theaters and attacked the film for promoting "perversion" and insulting Hindu religion. The mob violence was met with equally strong resistance from groups and individuals who opposed the Hindu Right's bigoted agenda. The widespread reporting of the controversy and the ensuing debate gave queer sexuality nationwide visibility. The *Fire* controversy led to independent India's first public debate on homosexuality and provided unprecedented visibility to queer people and

---

led many commentators to read it as an allegory for the love of human beings and God.

The *Ramayana* is an ancient Sanskrit epic that forms an important part of the Hindu canon. It is one of the two great epics of India, along with *Mahabharata*. The *Ramayana* tells the story of Ram (an incarnation of the Hindu preserver-god Vishnu), whose wife Sita is abducted by Ravana, the king of Lanka. There are several regional versions of the epic in India, as well as Thai, Lao, Burmese, and Malay versions. These versions often differ significantly from each other. Indian cinema and the performing arts refer frequently to both the *Ramayana* and *Mahabharata*.

4. Led by its political front, the Bharatiya Janata Party (BJP), the Hindu Right draws its ideological impetus from the parent organization, Rashtriya Swayamsevak Sangh (RSS) or the National Volunteer Organization. The more aggressive and militant factions include the Bajrang Dal (the Monkey Mob), the Vishwa Hindu Parishad (World Hindu Association), and the Shiv Sena (the Army of Shiva). The term Sangh Parivar (Family of Associations) refers to the various wings that are affiliated to the RSS. In this volume, I will refer to the Sangh Parivar as the Hindu Right.

activism. Queer sexuality had tumbled out of the closet and was in no mood to go back.

It is my contention that *Fire* is a decisive film for reasons that are beyond cinematic considerations. It is imperative that the film is understood not merely against universalist canons of "artistic merit," but by mapping it against a larger social and political history that was unfolding in the first decades of the new millennium. As feminist legal scholar Ratna Kapur has written:

> *Fire*, and the controversy that engulfed it, must be evaluated against [the] cultural contests and broader social antagonisms and contradictions that are being played out in the many cultural controversies that are erupting these days. The representation of sexual minorities, the inversion of cultural myths and themes, the agency of Hindu women within the joint family, all destabilize the understanding of culture, of Hindu culture, that is being put across by the Hindu Right. We need to take on board the fact that this is not just a freedom of speech struggle. It is an ideological struggle about who counts as part of Indian culture and who is excluded, an outsider. (Kapur 1999)

It is precisely at this discursive intersection that I will place my discussion of the film. As an Indian, Canadian, and South Asian diasporic project, *Fire* invites responses and readings from multiple locations and vantage points. To this end, my project is a partial one and is deeply inflected by my own location in India and my experience of the film at a particular historical moment.[5] Given that the "circulations, repressions and incitements" of *Fire* are "profoundly national and transnational," I have borne in mind during the writing of this volume Geeta Patel's good advice that the film needs to be "unpacked" for "a viewer unfamiliar with South Asia or a South-Asian viewer unfamiliar with Indian-language literature and cinema." The registers have to be translated so that the "alignments and gestures" can be seen (2002, 229). In the same way, I have tried to take seriously Gayatri Gopinath's excellent suggestion about resituating discussions of *Fire* "within discourses of non-heteronormative sexuality that are available to Indian and South Asian diasporic audiences" (1998, 633). This, she hopes, would challenge the "developmental narrative of modernity" that is premised on a notion of Western cultural superiority and "advanced politicization" (ibid).

The culture wars, however, did not end with *Fire*. The

---

5. The renaming of Bombay and Calcutta were undertaken as initiatives to preserve the identity, language, and culture of the ethnic majority when historically both cities have been inhabited by multi-ethnic and multi-religious populations. Many of us see the renaming as a non-cosmopolitan attempt to erase the multi-ethnic and multi-racial nomenclatural history of the cities. Therefore, I will continue to use the names Bombay (not Mumbai) and Calcutta (not Kolkata) in this volume.

ghosts of *Fire* rose from the ashes when Mehta returned to shoot *Water* in 2000. *Water* was meant to be Deepa Mehta's third film in the "Elements trilogy," after *Fire* and *Earth* (1998). Based on Pakistani writer Bapsi Sidhwa's *Ice Candy Man* (also titled *Cracking India*), *Earth* is about the demonic explosion of Hindu-Muslim rioting during the Partition of India. Since Mehta was never given permission to shoot on location in Lahore, in Pakistan, the entire film was shot instead in India. Set in 1938, *Water* (2005) is about the lives of four widows in Varanasi.[6] Jasbir Jain has written that the trilogy reflects Mehta's relationship with India, as it explores socio-cultural problems, patriarchal institutions such as marriage and the family, religious interventions in politics, and the politics of caste and gender (Jain 2009).

Mehta started preparing to shoot *Water* in January 2000 after the film was cleared by the Ministry of Information and Broadcasting. The female leads, as in *Fire*, were to be played by Shabana Azmi and Nandita Das, both of whom had shorn their hair to play the roles of the widows. Word got around that the film was a propaganda piece against the Hindu religion, and predictably the fanatics went on a rampage. Unruly mobs vandalized the sets and held demonstrations in the city. The number of protestors was not large, and a

6. Varanasi (also called Banaras or Kashi), a city in Uttar Pradesh, is situated on the banks of the river Ganges. Many Hindu widows were sent to live there when their husbands died. Religious Hindus, Buddhists, and Jains consider Varanasi a holy city.

FIGURE 2. The Hindu Right was determined to stop any project that brought Azmi, Das, and Mehta together. (Courtesy: Nandita Das)

highly publicized "suicide attempt" by a man turned out to be a sham, but using the surrounding furor as an excuse, the Uttar Pradesh state government stopped the shooting of the film. As the producers lost money with each passing day, the country witnessed the BJP-led government's inability to rein in their own foot soldiers. The film script traveled back to the Ministry, but nothing happened. Eventually the film had to be shelved. Several states (including Madhya Pradesh, Bihar, and Bengal) offered protection to Mehta and invited her to shoot in their states. She decided not to take their offers and returned to Canada. Later, the film was shot and completed in Sri Lanka with an entirely different cast and crew.[7] Having lost the battle of *Fire*, the Hindu Right took its revenge with *Water*. It was determined not to allow Shabana Azmi and Nandita Das to feature in a film together, especially one that was being made by Deepa Mehta, so the film ended up being censored even before it was made.

A less careful reading of the *Fire* and *Water* controversies runs the risk of being interpreted as a tussle between a (modern) progressive text and a (traditional) regressive society, and a majority of mainstream critics in the West (particularly in the US and Canada) saw them that way. These accounts paid little attention to the resilient counter-protests that witnessed widespread participation of leading industry professionals, writers, painters, artists, activists, feminists, queer rights activists, and people from all walks of life. For example, in the documentary *Filming Desire: A Journey through Women's Cinema* by Marie Mandy (2000), Deepa Mehta is introduced as follows: "Exiled in Toronto, Canada, [Deepa Mehta] condemns women's condition in India and is paying for it. When the film *Fire*, the first part of her trilogy *Fire*, *Earth*, *Water*, came out, the cinemas were set on fire by extremists. Her effigy was burnt throughout India. On the

---

7. It has remained a disappointment for many that *Water*, as originally conceived, was never made. *Water* is the only film in the trilogy that does not star Nandita Das and was not shot in India. When finally released in India in 2007, the film was met with no protest from the Hindu Right and little enthusiasm from others.

second day of shooting *Water*, a fire destroyed the entire set. Now she travels with six bodyguards."

Unfortunately, even the book written in 2006 by Deepa Mehta's daughter, Devyani Saltzman, reinforces this misconception. I hope this volume will contribute to challenging this singular construction and lay out instead the discursive complexity of the debate and the many narratives of resistance against the Hindu Right. After examining in detail the extra-textual consequences of the film, I will argue that *Fire* does make crucial cinematic interventions that have implications for both representational conventions and spectatorial practices.

Much has happened since the *Fire* controversy catapulted queer activism to new heights of public visibility in India with its demands for equality, inclusion, and sexual rights. In a historic judgment delivered on July 2, 2009, the Delhi High Court decriminalized non-heterosexual sex between consenting adults.[8] The judgment struck down section 377 of the Indian Penal Code (a colonial legislation drafted by Lord Macaulay in 1860) that criminalized and discriminated on the basis of sexual orientation. The queer community was euphoric. When Delhi held its first Queer Pride Parade in 2008 (whose original venue was the Regal Cinema, where the *Fire* protests had begun), Deepa Mehta was quoted as saying, "I wish I could be there. My heart swells with pride

---

8. *Naz Foundation v. Union of India.*

when *Fire* is mentioned as a favorite film. If it has inspired the homosexual community, I guess I have much to be proud of."[9] The matter is being heard in the Indian Supreme Court as of this writing in 2010 and, if it upholds the decision of the High Court, this will mark the greatest victory for those who dared to come out and/or came of age during the long battle catalyzed by the *Fire* controversy.

9. Deepa Mehta gets emotional about gay pride in Delhi, *India Abroad*, July 30, 2009. http://in.movies.yahoo.com/news-detail/28321/Deepa-Mehta-gets-emotional-gay-parade-in-Delhi.html#

ONE: BORN IN FLAMES

A brief history of production

"Deepa Mehta will travel only a few blocks on Bloor this evening from her little house in the Annex to the Varsity Theatre for the world Premiere of *Fire*," wrote Judy Gerstel of the *Toronto Star*. But the journey, as Gerstel accurately pointed out, was "neither short nor simple" (1996). In 1973, Deepa Mehta, then twenty-two years old, moved to Canada with her husband Paul Saltzman, a filmmaker and producer. The couple founded Sunrise Films, and Mehta established herself first as a documentary filmmaker and then moved into drama through her work on television. In 1991, she made her first feature film, *Sam and Me*. The film is about Nikhil, a young immigrant (Ranjit Chowdhry), who is forced by his overbearing sponsor uncle (Om Puri) to become a caregiver for Sam, an aging Jewish man (Peter Boretski) who has been emotionally abandoned by his career-driven son.[10] Despite their differences in race, class, religion, and age,

---

10. The story of *Sam and Me* is by Deepa Mehta; the screenplay is by Ranjit Chowdhry. *Sam and Me* also featured Kulbhushan Kharbanda and Jaaved Jaaferi, and all three actors worked in *Fire*. Mehta has consistently worked with the same crew, which includes Giles Nuttgens (cinematographer), Barry Farrell (editor), Anne Masson (line producer), and David Hamilton (producer). Mehta is currently married to Hamilton.

Sam and Nik become close. The intimacy between the two is resented by both families, who intercede to separate the pair. This moving film inaugurates many of the themes that Mehta developed in her later work, including the trauma of migration, the tensions of multiculturalism, the challenges of loneliness, and the promise of friendship in seemingly impossible situations. She also introduces what would later become recurrent themes in her films—homosocial bonding, possibilities of same-sex eroticism, and the subversive potential of drag performances.

Sam and Me won the Camera d'Or ("Golden Camera") prize at the Cannes Film Festival. Ironically, at the same time she was receiving fame and recognition, Mehta's marriage was falling apart. Through a period of unsettling personal crises, Mehta started building a professional life for herself. She was picked up by George Lucas to direct two episodes of the television series *The Young Indiana Jones Chronicles*. In 1994, she got a big break when she was invited to direct her first major film, the UK-Canada co-production *Camilla*, a buddy-bonding film starring Jessica Tandy and Bridget Fonda. The so-called big break turned out to be a hard lesson in big-budget filmmaking when Mehta was denied the director's cut; the project was taken from her hands and re-edited. The film flopped. It was during this moment of crisis, when she gave herself up as professionally dead, that the idea for the film *Fire* came to her.

In April 1995, Mehta was sitting in a cottage in Ontario

and staring at the frozen lake outside. Suddenly, the colors of *Fire* appeared before her. "I knew it was going to be orange, white and green, the colors of the Indian flag."[11] Looking at the snow outside, she imagined the opening sequence of the film: a young newlywed couple contemplate the Taj Mahal on a sultry summer day. The story she wanted to tell was one about the rapid changes in India following the liberalization of the economy, a story that would demystify the "exotic" India and foreground the conflicts of contemporary urban life. More specifically, she would explore how contemporary women were negotiating the tensions between duty and desire. The film, she hoped, would be both a portrait of contemporary life and an allegory.

"I started thinking of a house in Delhi and its inhabitants," says Mehta. "A woman comes into an arranged marriage, and I thought of a sister-in-law, of course, because there are lots of them around. There are [joint] families all across India. Then it was a matter of interaction between them and [defining] what their husbands were like. It developed from characters rather than the story itself" (Cuthbert, 1996).[12]

---

11. Gerstel, Judy. FilmFest '96. Canadians kick it off. *The Star*. September 6, 1996. http://www.thestar.com/editorial/filmfest/960906D01a_MO-MEHTA06.html.

12. Mehta was to revisit this theme in *Heaven on Earth* (2008), a film that has many resonances with *Fire*. When a young migrant bride is faced with cruelty and violence in her husband's home, she

The central conflicts played out in *Fire* were issues close to Mehta's heart. She thought of her mother and aunts who had arranged marriages and faced the consequences. Mehta recalled: "[*Fire*] grew out of the many complex events I saw in the unfolding of [the] arranged marriages of my mother and her sisters. In each case these vibrant, intelligent women left the comfort and security of their homes to be subsumed by the unfamiliar environment of virtual strangers. Their radical adjustment to an unknown husband and the assumption of his family as their own was not done without difficulty. It often took them many years to adjust" (Comer 1997).

To make this film, she would have to return home to India, a move she compares with Neil Jordan's return to Ireland in order to make *The Crying Game* (1992). When Mehta decided to cast Indian actors in the film, the project was immediately disqualified for official Canadian funding and a guarantee of Canadian distribution, but she did not want to compromise the film by shooting it in Canada. Eventually, Mehta managed to raise the money for the film through pri-

---

invokes the fable of Sheshnaag, the mythical snake who comes to her rescue. Both films are about migrant brides (Sita comes to Delhi from Kanpur, while *Heaven*'s Chand goes to Brampton, Ontario, from Punjab). They suffer alienating marriages and transform their lives through the power of desire. The women in both films undergo tradition-inspired tests of purity whose outcome allows them to become custodians of their own destiny. "Tradition" in Mehta's films can be both oppressive and liberating.

vate sources; ninety percent of the funding came from Canadian investors and the rest from Indian. Once the funds were
in place, Mehta went to India to start casting for the film.

"People always want to know why I chose such a controversial film as my first film," said Nandita Das. "It's simply
because I didn't know there was going to be a second film."[13]
Das had acted in a TV serial but was not looking to build a
career in acting. In November 1995, actor Gulshan Grover
(best known for his villainous roles in Bombay films) suggested that Nandita meet a Canadian director called Deepa
Mehta who was auditioning actresses for a very "bold" film.
"Nobody used the word lesbian or even homosexual at the
time," recalls Das. "The film was always described through
euphemisms like 'bold' and 'unconventional'" (ibid). Das
went to meet Mehta at the hotel, and the first thing she no-
ticed when she entered the room was Mehta's sari. "Isn't that
from Fabindia?" she asked. "I have one exactly like that."
Mehta looked up to see Das and later said that she knew
right then she had found her Sita. Das and Mehta struck up
an immediate rapport. Describing their first meeting, Mehta
wrote: "We spend hours talking and I know at once that this
is the Sita I've been searching for in Toronto, New York,
London, and finally Bombay. No need for a screen test. I see
the tape of a serial she's the lead in. Not only is she a superb
actress, but the camera loves her" (Mehta 1996).

13. Interview with the author on March 26, 2010.

Mehta always knew that she wanted to cast Shabana Azmi for the role of Radha.[14] Shabana Azmi is arguably India's most versatile and talented actress. Her international reputation far exceeds that of any of her contemporaries. A known activist and a Member of Parliament's upper house, the Rajya Sabha, Azmi was initially reluctant to act in the film as she was unsure about how playing such a role would affect her political life.[15] She discussed the issue with her husband, Javed Akhtar, one of Bombay's most respected scriptwriters, poets, and lyricists, and he persuaded her to take the role. Once the decision was made, she was completely committed to the project. Mehta was exultant, convinced that only Shabana could do justice to the role of Radha, who had to

---

14. Shabana Azmi (b. 1950) made her debut in Shyam Benegal's *Ankur* (*Seedling*) in 1974, a film which pioneered the Indian New Wave film movement of the 1970s and 1980s. Having acted in innumerable New Wave films, Azmi became one of its most significant authors. In a spectacular career spanning parallel, art house, regional, and popular cinema, Azmi built a formidable national and international reputation as an actress. She has worked with almost every leading director in the country, including Satyajit Ray, and has won the National Film Award five times, along with nearly every acting award in India.

15. Azmi is also a highly respected social activist who has fought for the rights of construction laborers, slum dwellers, and other minority groups. She was nominated to the Rajya Sabha (India's upper House of the Parliament) by the President of India and served from 1997 to 2003.

"unleash her demons with dignity, not with hysteria." Mehta had considered other very talented actresses in the interim, but no one seemed to have Shabana's "inner strength and quiet purity."[16]

Mehta's cinematographer for *Fire* was Giles Nuttgens, with whom she had previously collaborated on shooting the Lucasfilm TV series *The Young Indiana Jones Chronicles*.[17] Mehta was drawn to Nuttgens' "bizarre and beautiful style" style, especially his use of white highlights (Comer 1997), and she saw that, because he had worked in India, he understood the quality of the light there. Nuttgens and Mehta were agreed on the color scheme. The film would be suffused with warm colors, as blue tones, which worked well for many films set in colder countries, would be completely unsuitable to this film. They also decided not to use gels. Aradhana Seth, who had worked with them on the *Indiana Jones* series, came on board as production designer. She had the task of evolving and implementing the color palette and of creating the spaces in which the story would be staged.

---

16. Notes from the Director's Diary. 1996. *Fire* Press Kit (courtesy Nandita Das, and on file with the author).

17. Giles Nuttgens became a cameraperson at a very young age. He shot his first feature film, *Electric Moon*, in India in 1992. Nuttgens spent four years shooting George Lucas's internationally known *Young Indiana Jones Chronicles*.

FIGURE 3. Deepa Mehta and Giles Nuttgens on location. (Courtesy: Nandita Das)

In the film, the extended family of the Kapurs lives in Lajpat Nagar, a bustling middle-class neighborhood in South Delhi where residential houses and shops stand cheek-by-jowl. For the purposes of shooting, Seth created the Kapur house by combining three different locations. The film required three separate spaces: the living spaces within the apartment; a big terrace overlooking the neighborhood; and a ground-floor area that would house the family business. The interiors were shot in a fairly small apartment in Sarita Vihar, a South Delhi colony quieter than Lajpat Nagar. The downstairs area, which houses the family business of video rentals and takeout food, was constructed and shot on location in Lajpat Nagar. At one end of this area, Seth created a "'cheat" staircase that would lead upstairs to the apartment. The third space—the expansive terrace—was shot in yet another location in Lajpat Nagar. The view from the terrace is what establishes the busy and congested locale in which the apartment is situated.

Because the filming would take place in a very small apartment, several handheld shoots were necessary. For this, Nuttgens chose a versatile lightweight Arriflex camera that could be outfitted with 35 and 18mm prime lenses. Since Mehta does not use storyboards, she likes to choreograph scenes and rehearse them with her actors prior to shooting. It was during this process that Nuttgens and Mehta decided that they wanted the camera to move constantly but unobtrusively.

During the shooting of the film, the team had to overcome several obstacles. By the time the film went into pre-production, all lights and lighting fixtures in the busy film center of Bombay had already been hired out, so the crew had to import lights from the UK. Shooting in the different locations that the script demanded did not prove to be easy either. Locations that had been promised for shooting would suddenly be canceled, and the crew and cast would have to quickly adapt to new locations. Notwithstanding the many hitches, not unusual for film shoots in India, the team managed to complete the shooting within a hectic thirty-day schedule.

Once *Fire* was completed, a new dilemma surfaced. Ironically, it had to do with the nationality of the film. Was *Fire* a Canadian film or was it an Indian film? Although its entire cast and much of the crew was Indian, *Fire* had been funded by private producers in both countries, and officially the governments of neither country had a role to play. But the Toronto International Film Festival invited Mehta to inaugurate their opening night in 1996, thereby positioning the film as Canadian. The debates around the nationality of the project raised a conflict for Mehta: what do national cultures mean to migrant artists? Was she an Indian director or a Canadian director? Did it even matter? When asked how Mehta viewed herself, she quoted a character from Salman Rushdie's story collection *East, West*. A boy is asked whether he is Indian or British. His answer is, "I refuse to choose" (Lacey 1997).

The changing mediascape of the 1990s

In order to understand why the explosive controversy surrounding *Fire* unleashed such fierce opposition and support, it is important to understand the context and the historical circumstances that led up to the release of the film. The early 1990s witnessed three major developments in India that had far-reaching consequences. In 1991, the Congress Party-led government confronted a severe economic crisis by initiating a widespread restructuring of the economy with globalization as its main imperative. This was accompanied by an "open sky" policy that initiated and accelerated the proliferation of satellite television.[18] These two developments ran parallel to what was perhaps the darkest phenomenon of the time—the rise of the Hindu Right led by its political front, the Bharatiya Janata Party (BJP). On December 6, 1992, supporters and allies of the Hindu Right demolished the Babri Masjid, a medieval mosque in Ayodhya in the state of Uttar Pradesh, claiming that it had been built on a temple destroyed by the invading Muslim king Babur. The Mosque-Temple confrontation resulted in widespread communal tension that unleashed rioting and violence across the country. Bombay, home of the Shiv Sena, witnessed the systematic persecution and killing of Muslims.[19] The demolition of the Babri Masjid isolated the BJP momentarily in Parliament but eventually propelled its rise to political power. In 1996, the BJP came to power for only thirteen days, but in 1998, with the support of splinter parties, it formed the government. The BJP-led coalition called themselves

18. Throughout the 1970s and 1980s, India was in the vanguard of the call for a New World Information and Communication Order. Anxieties around cultural imperialism and the domination of western news organizations resulted in a closed broadcasting system, consonant with India's closed economic system (Sinha 1998, 22).

19. In March 1995, the BJP-Shiv Sena alliance formed the government in Maharashtra.

the National Democratic Alliance (NDA).[20] The Hindu Right's rise to power coincided with the disintegration of the Congress Party and the growth of regional parties that came to power in some states.[21]

The post-liberalization mediascape of the 1990s was born on the cusp of deep anxieties and great expectations. Throughout the country, the rapid proliferation of satellite television and cable networks in the early years of the decade quickly dismantled the state's monopoly over television, providing urban audiences with a wide variety of local and imported programming. The technological and structural changes had a dramatic impact on the cultural practices of the urban elite. In this vastly transformed urban environment, the boundaries between film, television, and streaming videos collapsed. This new and accelerated flow of images into urban middle-class homes triggered both hope and anxiety. The popular discourse around the "opening of the skies" was replete with combative imagery that frequently used expressions like "assault," "onslaught," and "invasion."

---

20. The NDA lost the elections in 2004, and a Congress-led coalition formed the government. The same coalition won the elections in 2009.

21. The Indian National Congress (Congress Party) was founded in 1885 and spearheaded the movement for India's independence. Its famous leaders included Mahatma Gandhi and Jawaharlal Nehru, India's first Prime Minister.

Consequently, satellite TV was seen to cause deviant acts while eroding the "culture and tradition" of India. This anxiety manifested itself in demands for stringent legislation, greater censorship, and even demands for a ban on satellite TV. Paradoxically, public apprehensions were matched by an equally intense and unprecedented engagement with television.

The Hindu Right opposed satellite TV on the grounds that it threatened Indian culture and values while promoting westernization. Their rise to power was accompanied by an aggressive cultural nationalism that invoked the specter of Indian culture being threatened by marauding forces of foreign origin. Their cultural interventions included violent attacks on speech and representation that they considered "vulgar and obscene" or simply deemed hurtful to "Hindu sentiments." Most often, the targets of attacks were speech and the representation of women's bodies that, while maintaining continuities with various traditions of iconography, transgressed the more traditional notions of womanhood.

However, the moral panics that marked the decade of the 1990s, while initiated by the Hindu Right, was not exclusive to them. Many secular organizations, including women's groups, articulated concerns around the emergence of satellite television, in a manner that often dangerously overlapped with the anxieties of the Hindu Right.[22] Despite their

---

22. See People's Perceptions: Obscenity and Violence on the

ideological differences, both the Hindu Right and some women's organizations frequently targeted the same representations and demanded similar censorious measures.[23] Feminists, while avoiding the use of the term censorship, advocated limits on speech and expression by deploying terms such as "reasonable restrictions," "control," and "regulation." The differences between these recommendations and the demands for censorship were never made clear.

The 1990s in India were also characterized by a series of crackdowns on representations of sex and sexuality. In 1993, the BJP and Shiv Sena launched an attack on Bombay cinema, alleging that the films bore witness to the "deterioration of film culture" and were replete with "insults to the Hindu faith," "promotion of anti-national elements," and "body ex-

---

Small Screen, a study by the Media Advocacy Group (MAG). 1994. Formed in 1992, the main objective of the MAG was to monitor and conduct public interest research on the mass media. This particular study was commissioned by the Indian National Commission for Women. Later, MAG was formalized as the Centre for Advocacy and Research (CFAR) See also 'Six bad apples spoil the whole bunch', Nikhat Kazmi, *Times of India*, May 15, 1994.

23. Secular women's groups have consistently critiqued women's subordination in traditional family and cultural values, while the Hindu Right predictably insists on women's traditional role in the family and looks on feminism itself as an assault on women's traditional values.

posure" [*sic*].[24] This was followed by a series of public attacks on speech and representation deemed to be obscene and vulgar. The first such controversy broke out over the song "Choli Ke Peechey Kya Hai" ("What's Behind the Blouse?") from the film *Khalnayak* (*The Villain*, Subhash Ghai, 1993). The Shiv Sena and the ABVP (the student wing of the BJP) led the protest against the song, which led to a petition being filed in the Delhi high court asking for the deletion of the song from the film and a ban on audiocassette sales as the song was allegedly "vulgar" and "against public morality and decency."[25] Next in the line of attacks were film songs like "*Sexy, Sexy, Sexy Mujhe Log Boley*" ("People Say I Am Sexy, Sexy, Sexy") from *Khuddar* (*Man of Integrity*, Iqbal Durrani, 1993) and "*Meri Pant Bhi Sexy*" ("My Pants Are Sexy") from the film *Dulara (The Loved One*, Nikhil Vinay, 1993). The word "sexy" got both films in trouble. In the case of *Dulara*, the word "sexy" was replaced with "fancy," while in the case of *Khuddar*, the word was replaced with "baby" But the original "sexy" versions never stopped circulating, and so both songs went onto become chartbusters.

Organizations that protested against the "obscenity and vulgarity" of film songs included the National Human Rights

---

24. Clash: That's entertainment, that's politics. 1993. *Filmfare*. Juy.

25. The petition argued that increasing obscenity and vulgarity in public life would lead to an increase in sexual harassment. In a fourteen-page order, the High Court dismissed the petition.

Commission (NHRC), the Centre for Media Studies, the National Commission for Women (NCW), the Parliamentary Standing Committee, and the Central Board of Film Certification (CBFC, commonly referred to as the Censor Board). In 1994, the CBFC recommended ten substantive cuts in Shekhar Kapur's film *Bandit Queen* for its depiction of sex and violence, and the Shiv Sena launched its "clean up culture" drive in their stronghold, the state of Maharashtra, designed to save Indian culture from sexual permissiveness. In 1995, a Chelsea Jeans advertisement started a controversy with the ad copy "F*** Off! Leave Us Alone." The accompanying photograph first showed two men standing in intimate proximity, then, in a later version, two women in leather and jeans in a similar pose. While the ad featuring the men passed without much comment, the one featuring the two women created a commotion. Responding to protests from certain women's groups, the Ad Standards Council and the Advertising Agencies Association of India ensured that the ad was withdrawn. While admitting to not having seen it, the president of the latter organization condemned the "obscene advertisement" and criticized the publications that carried it (Singh 1995).

The year 1996 witnessed a rapid succession of public denunciations. In January, the Shiv Sena launched an offensive against an advertisement for Tuff shoes that showed a nude couple (featuring star models Madhu Sapre and Milind Soman) locked in an embrace with a snake wrapped around their necks. In April 1996, filmmaker Mahesh Bhatt was publicly castigated for suggesting that people living in a democracy had the right to watch pornography if they wished.[26] Several important women's groups demanded his ouster from the governing council of the prestigious Film and Television Institute of India (FTII) and, in a memorandum submitted to the Information and Broadcasting Ministry, declared that anyone who held such a view about pornography was not fit to hold an important office. The memorandum argued further that while the constitutional provision of free speech and expression were important, imposing "reasonable restrictions" were imperative to prevent practices that were "derogatory to the dignity of women." It demanded "a code of decency" aimed at checking the aforesaid obscenity and vulgarity in the media. During its thirteen-day reign of power, the Minister of Information and Broadcasting, Sushma Swaraj, warned women newscasters not to wear "semi-transparent" clothes. Swaraj banned an advertisement for a music system that showed a woman's skirt billowing to the music and banned a sex education program that she felt would promote "adultery."

In January 1997, the extremist Hindu group Bajrang Dal

26. Mahesh Bhatt is one of Bombay's most outspoken and progressive filmmakers. He achieved fame with *Arth* (*Meaning*, 1982), starring Shabana Azmi, which became a feminist cult classic. His *Tamanna* (*Longing*, 1997) was one of the first popular films from Bombay to have a transgender person as the central protagonist.

attacked the M.F. Husain, India's most famous painter for his line drawing of the Hindu goddess Saraswati. This drawing, one of the many stylized female nudes in his repertoire, was made in 1976 but reproduced in a BJP-backed magazine to accompany an article that attacked the Muslim painter for denigrating Hinduism. Even though the attack was communally motivated, it used the rhetoric of anti-obscenity campaigns.[27]

I have described this sequence of events in some detail to demonstrate that the controversy over *Fire* emerged at the confluence of several currents. It is important to note that the attacks by the Hindu Right and the demands for restrictions on speech did not go unchallenged. Every controversy was met with increasingly vocal counter-protests insisting that it was imperative to uphold the constitutional guarantee of freedom of speech and expression. Given the repeated incidents of censorious righteousness that preceded the release of the film, the Hindu Right's attack on *Fire* was almost predictable. What was not expected was the overwhelming

---

27. According to the *Merriam-Webster Dictionary*, "communalism" denotes "social organization on a communal basis" or "loyalty to a socio-political grouping based on religious or ethnic affiliation." In South Asia, however, communalism denotes the attempt to promote narrow identity-based interests by mobilizing religious identities. In this volume, communalism refers primarily to the chauvinistic, anti-Muslim politics of Hindu Right groups.

support the film would receive and the vibrant public debate on homosexuality that it would lead to.

I have elsewhere written that these events were manifestations of a public anxiety around the shifting moral framework around issues of sexuality (Ghosh 1999c). By contributing to the creation of a moralistic and censorious public culture, pro-censorship feminists had endangered the already shrinking space for the expression of women's sexuality. The feminist interventions in the controversies around vulgarity and obscenity seemed to conclude that all (or any) speech and representation of sex and sexuality were problematic, blurring the distinctions between coercion and consent, sexism and sexual explicitness. Predictably, pro-censorship feminists legitimized demands for the deletion of all sexual representation, regardless of whether it existed within a discourse of violence, sexism, or misogyny. In her response to John and Niranjana, Ratna Kapur pointed out that many of the lesbian representatives who were protesting the cancellation of the screening of *Fire* had "either not supported or seen to be visibly supporting the rights of other sexually marginalized communities." On the contrary, they had "taken a contradictory stand on the issue of free expression in the context of other films/film songs that have been banned or restricted" (1999). Consequently, lesbians had served as "barricades against free speech rather than its active promoters." There is no doubt that the feminist confusion and ambivalence around issues of free speech and sexual minorities helped prepare the ground on which the fierce opposition to *Fire* would be staged.

On the other hand, the 1990s also witnessed an efflorescence of sexual speech in the electronic and print media. Transgressive ideas frequently emerged on the margins before making their way into mainstream popular culture. Riyad Wadia's independent, experimental film *BomGay* (1996) inaugurated queer-identified films in India. Starring the now-popular actor Rahul Bose, *BomGay*, a highly stylized avant-garde film structured around six poems by R. Raj Rao, circulated widely in queer circles and international film festivals. Wadia's next film, *A Mermaid Called Aida* (1996), is a feature-length documentary on well-known transsexual Aida Banaji. Like most documentaries, both films circulated widely through an expansive network of non-commercial screenings.[28]

The films of Pratibha Parmar, a UK-based filmmaker of Indian origin, also exerted considerable influence on the emergent gay and lesbian movement in India. From the mid-1980s, Parmar made films about queer South Asians and their concerns. *Khush* (*Happy*, 1991), a short documenta-

---

28. Like many independent filmmakers in India (especially documentary and experimental filmmakers), Wadia never submitted his films for censor certification. Their explicit references to homosexuality would have never been cleared by censors. Even today, many independent documentary filmmakers who work on controversial themes choose not to submit their films to the CBFC.

ry exploring queer South Asian identities, won many awards and is now a cult classic. Her films include *Sari Red* (1988), a video poem about the violence faced by South Asian women, and *Flesh and Paper* (1990), an experimental film on lesbian writer Suniti Namjoshi. *A Place of Rage* (1991) is about the struggles and achievement of African-American women, and features Angela Davis, June Jordan, and Alice Walker. Her other films include *Double the Trouble Twice the Fun* (1992), about gay people with disabilities, featuring writer Firdaus Kanga and *Jodie* (1996) about actress Jodie Foster's transatlantic status as a gay icon. Almost single-handedly, Parmar has traversed a wide range of formal devices and styles to address the many concerns of South Asian queers in the diaspora. Working both from the margins and the center, Parmar introduced non-mainstream ideas into the mainstream.[29] Mainstream films like *Daayraa* (*The Square Circle*, Amol Palekar, 1997), *Darmiyaan: In Between* (Kalpana Lazmi, 1997), and *Tamanna* (*Longing*) had queer central protagonists.

During the 1990s, satellite TV's many narratives had also begun to make space for queer representations and the interrogation of heteronormativity. Issues of queer sexuality were directly addressed on newscasts, talk shows, and

---

29. In 2006, Parmar released her first feature film, *Nina's Heavenly Delights*, about a Scottish Indian woman struggling to retain a family restaurant. In this self-confident and cheerful film, queer identities are not a problem but a part of everyday life.

interviews. TV drama and sitcoms concurrently introduced characters who, though not explicitly designated as gay or lesbian, were unmistakably queer in that they challenged commonplace assumptions of sexual normativity. Queerness was also emerging in the larger public culture through popular magazines, theater, dance, and other cultural forms.[30]

For the first time, Indian films and TV began foregrounding a theme that had hitherto remained underrepresented—female bonding. Television serials such as *Adhikar (Rights)*, *Mujhe Chand Chahiye (I Want the Moon)*, *Kabhi Kabhi (Once in a While)*, and *Hasratein (Desires)* depicted female friendships of varying intensity. In *Mujhe Chand Chahiye*, a young girl falls in love with a woman teacher. One of the longest running and critically acclaimed serials, *Adhikar*, revolves around the relationship between a Muslim woman Shama, and a Hindu woman, Amita. Their male partners notwithstanding, the relationship between the two women remains the most privileged. In one episode, for example, after Amita has fearlessly testified in a rape trial, the women are alone in a room. The sequence begins with Amita and Shama gazing

30. Urban Indian English-language theater has a tradition of representing queerness on stage that dates back to at least the late 1970s. In the 1990s, there was a greater proliferation of such plays, including those of gay dramatist Mahesh Dattani, Rustom Bharucha's Hindi adaptation of Manuel Puig's *Kiss of the Spider Woman* (1993), and Barry John's *Varun* (1993). In 1994–95, Shantanu Nagpal produced the play *O Bulky Stomach*.

into each other's eyes. Amita raises her mouth and blows
a kiss to a delighted Shama. The conversation proceeds as
follows:

Shama: "You are unmatched. Only you could have
said what you did in that crowded courtroom. When
I look at you, I wonder—what am I? I am probably
beautiful, my complexion is fair—what else do I have?
But look at you—I so feel like kissing you."

Amita: "Don't! You'll spoil me. [My boyfriend] has
already kissed me."

Shama: "What? You shameless woman …"

Amita: "Why shameless? If he doesn't kiss me on
such an occasion ..."

Shama: "What nonsense you speak."

Amita: "Even when I speak nonsense, I speak the
truth. Really—if I were a man, I swear, I would have
married you."

Shama [laughing]: "Earlier, I only suspected it but
now it's confirmed."

Amita: "What?"

Shama: "That you are not a woman. There is nothing woman-like in you. There is a man inside you."

Amita: "Wah! How well you have spoken. That's precisely the point, my friend. You have described me absolutely right. Now, what prize should I give you? Should I kiss you?" [leans over and kisses her on her lips]

Amita: "There, I've kissed you."

Shama: "You've polluted me!" [laughs in delight]

Amita: "Pollution is part of our religion–not yours. You people drink from the same cup."

Shama: "I don't want to drink from everyone's cup."

Amita: "Not everyone—just two!" [holds up two fingers]

Shama "Two?"

Amita: "Yes. First it was only me. [Your husband] arrived much later."

Shama [amused, looks toward the door of the room to see if anyone has heard]: "Idiot! You don't care about your own reputation. At least care about mine." [She gets up and shuts the door, then returns and sits in front of Amita.] "What would have happened if someone had heard?"

Ironically, the protests meant to suppress sexual speech only ended up circulating it. In the case of the Chelsea Jeans advertisement, for example, the attack only served to highlight its contents. Through its multiple genres, TV pushed the boundaries of heteronormativity by challenging the certitudes around monogamy, marriage, and heterosexuality. Just as dissident speech around heterosexuality challenged its compulsory location within marriage and monogamy, queer sexuality challenged heterosexuality itself. This discursive conversation found space on film, in television, print, and cyberspace, in real conversations, and in tentative whispers. Public culture in India was beginning to witness a gradual coming out of queer sexuality. But it was only with *Fire* that the first debate on homosexuality entered public life.

The film's release and attendant controversy

On December 2, 1998, six years after the demolition of the Babri Mosque, fanatics of the Hindu Right went on a rampage against *Fire*. The film had been released all over India on November 13, 1998, and had been running to fairly packed houses. The protests against the film began gradually. On November 25, a little-known group in Bombay called the Jain Vahini Samiti threatened to disrupt screenings if the film was not officially banned. Six days later, an eight-member delegation of the Mahila Aghadi (the women's wing

of the Shiv Sena) met cultural affairs minister Pramod Navalkar and submitted a petition demanding a ban on the film.
The petition read: "If women's physical needs get fulfilled
through lesbian acts, the institution of marriage will collapse
… reproductions of human beings will stop." (Writer Man-
jula Padmanabhan retorted that, given the "rate at which
Indians reproduce," this could well be "the single most powerful argument in favour of lesbianism!")[31] A leader of the
Aghadi told Navalkar that since "a majority of the women in
our society do not even know about lesbianism, why expose
them to it?" Navalkar duly forwarded the letter to the prime
minister and the head of the Censor Board.

The next day, Shiv Sena activists in Bombay barged into
Cinemax theater in suburban Goregaon and started burning
posters and smashing glass windows. The agitators managed
to stop the afternoon screening of *Fire* and forced the theater authorities to refund the ticket money to the audience.
New Empire, the other Bombay theater in which the film
was showing, canceled screenings in anticipation of attacks.
Instead of condemning the vandalism, the chief minister of
in the state of Maharashtra, Manohar Joshi, lauded the activists for trying to stop a film whose "theme was alien to our
culture."[32] The owner of the Cinemax told the *Times of India*:

31. *Pioneer*, December 13, 1998.

32. *Fire* pulled out of cinema halls, *Pioneer*, December 3, 1998.

"We could not continue to screen the film after the chief minister congratulated the mob which stormed the theater and damaged our premises. If we continue with the shows there is danger of members of the audience losing their lives for which we will held to be responsible."[33]

On December 3, a mob of Shiv Sena workers attacked Regal Cinema in Delhi's Connaught Place. The film was showing to packed houses when an unruly mob began to tear down the posters and destroy property. Both the theater management and audiences were taken by surprise because nobody had seen the mob arrive; they had arrived unobtrusively and mingled with audiences waiting to enter the theater. At about 12:45 pm, they whipped out yellow scarves, tied them around their necks, and embarked on a spree of destruction which ended up damaging a nearby restaurant that had nothing to do with the film. The vandals forced their way into the manager's office where, after fifteen minutes of mayhem and extensive damage to property, the mob dispersed. The show continued after the disruption, but the subsequent three shows were canceled. The other cinema halls that were screening the film canceled their shows for fear of mob violence. Jai Bhagwan Goyal, chief of the Delhi Shiv Sena branch, gloated over the success of the campaign and threatened more such attacks if the film continued to be

---

33. *Times of India*, December 4, 1998.

screened. "This is just the trailer," he declared. "We will not let them run such films which damage society."[33]

The attack on *Fire* did not go unchallenged. Writers, artists, filmmakers, politicians, and the general public were quick to condemn the actions of the Shiv Sena. Scriptwriter Javed Akhtar (husband of actress Shabana Azmi) denounced the destructive protests. Filmmaker Mahesh Bhatt, whose courageous film on communalism *Zakhm* (*The Wound*, 1998) had been censored by the CFBC, said *Fire* was not "ugly or vulgar" but a sensitive work dealing with a "heritage of humankind." Both Azmi and Das were trenchant in their criticism of the attacks. Azmi expressed shock that a small group of people had hijacked law and order; *Asian Age* quoted her as saying that "[t]hose who have a problem need not see the film, but they must not be allowed to interfere with the people who do."[34]

Meanwhile, Parliament was in an uproar over the *Fire* controversy. Eminent journalist Kuldeep Nayyar condemned the Maharashtra government's support of the vandals. Shiv Sena MP Pritish Nandy, former editor of the now-defunct but well-respected periodical, *Illustrated Weekly of India*, took issue with Nayyar. He claimed that if "alternative sexuality" was to be given space, the same privilege should be extended to "alternative politics." This reference was to a ban on a play about Gandhi's assassin, Nathuram Godse. Nandy de-

34. *Asian Age*, December 4, 1998.

clared that one should not "make heroes and heroines out of assassins and lesbians" so as not to make "murder and sexual deviation [*sic*] heroic." He urged the "august house" to refrain from intervening so that the matter could be sorted out by the "women's wings of different political parties."[35]

The BJP-led government refused to take action against the Shiv Sena. Instead, they targeted the film as the source of all trouble and defended the vandalism by stating that freedom of speech and expression did not mean that "anything could be shown." In an entirely unprecedented decision, the Ministry of Information and Broadcasting referred the film back to the CBFC. For the first time in the history of Indian cinema, a certified film had been sent back for re-examination.

On December 6, activists of the Hindu Right made a futile attempt to disrupt the screening of *Fire* at a theater in Calcutta, but the attempt was foiled when angry audiences chased the hooligans away. The next day, a group of well-known Bombay citizens filed a petition in the Supreme Court urging the chief justice to demand from the Maharashtra government an explanation for its failure to provide protection at the screening of *Fire*. Petitioners included Javed Akhtar, filmmakers Yash Chopra and Mahesh Bhatt, retired lawyer and judge Atul Setalvad, his daughter, human

---

35. Much heat in Rajya Sabha over *Fire*. *The Statesman*. December 4, 1998.

rights activist and journalist Teesta Setalvad, veteran actor Dilip Kumar, and several others. The petition named as its respondents Shiv Sena chief Bal Thackeray and Chief Minister Manohar Joshi.

At the same time, a small group of writers, filmmakers, artists, feminists, human rights activists, and gays and lesbians held a peaceful protest in front of the Regal Cinema. Those of us who had gathered there that day had no idea that the demonstration would receive so much support from people on the streets. I remember a young woman, who held the hand of a toddler, approaching us. "What are you protesting against?" she asked with a smile. After listening to us, she asked: "Do you mind if we join?" A retired police officer told me that day that he was upset about how blatantly the Shiv Sena had taken the law into their own hands. Quite a few people gathered to listen to our conversation, and many agreed with us. The discontent with the Hindu Right's cultural policing was palpable.

The debate over *Fire* also dominated the print and electronic media. Condemning Shiv Sena's vandalism, an editorial in the *Pioneer* on December 4, 1998 entitled "War on Culture" asserted that "vitriolic, often violent, outbursts against the threat of 'cultural invasion' are a frequent manifestation of the Shiv Sena brand of politics, [and] the violent protest against the screening of Deepa Mehta's award-winning film *Fire* ... is certainly the most reprehensible." As a letter to the editor in the *Indian Express* (December 8,

1998) asked: "How can our society allow a small group of rowdies to decide what may or may not be screened? Why should the large silent majority be deprived of seeing what they wish to see and what the relevant authority, the Censor Board has approved?" More importantly, taboo words such as "homosexuals" and "lesbians" had begun to enter everyday conversation. The word lesbian had moved from the dark recesses of marginality to the illuminated center of public discourse. This journey was eloquently described by a lesbian activist who, in a dossier compiled for the Campaign for Lesbian Rights, said:

> By the morning of December 8 it had all happened.
> The word "lesbian" was on the front pages of every
> newspaper I picked up in Delhi. LESBIAN. It
> looked odd and out of place. Why was a word like
> that being tossed around? A word so loaded with
> fear, embarrassment, prejudice, a word shrouded
> in silence, a whisper that spoke of an identity that
> must be hidden from others, that frightening word
> that dare not cross any threshold, was on that
> winter morning landing at the doorstep of millions
> of households in many parts of the country. At my
> colleagues' doors. At my parent's. At my neighbors'.
> At my landlord's. My neighbor was going to read it.
> The Mother Dairy man was going to read it. The
> woman in the workshop. My sister-in-law … They

were all going to pick up the morning newspaper and
stare at a word that they had possibly not seen earlier
in print, and never given much thought to, and
wonder what it was doing on Page One. And Three.
And in editorials. And in letters to editors. And in
special Features. Not just that day but for days and
weeks and weeks after December 8. (S.L. 1999)

On December 9, the Supreme Court declined to provide
security to the producers of *Fire* and instead fixed a date to
hear a plea by a Bombay residents' association that sought to
demand an apology from the makers of *Fire* for affronting
Hindu sentiments by portraying lesbians in a Hindu household. On the same day, thirty counter-protestors carrying
placards that read "Keep off Cricket and Culture" con-
vened in front of Bombay's New Empire theater. The police
were quick to round up the demonstrators and arrest them.
Meanwhile, the Congress Party had roused itself to declare
support for the film and made a scathing attack on the Shiv
Sena. They urged people who disagreed with the contents
of the film not to resort to violence but take their grievances
to the courts. The National Commission of Women also issued a statement condemning the Shiv Sena's "violence and
vandalism." A few days later, the Shiv Sena tried to provide
a new impetus to their agitation by adopting a unique mode
of protest. About sixty Shiv Sena activists stripped down
to their underwear and held a demonstration outside actor
Dilip Kumar's house. This underwear demonstration was a

protest against what they saw as nudity in *Fire*. For those who struggled to decipher the connection, a leader helpfully explained: "[Kumar] has spoken out [in favor] of individual rights and, in a way, supported nudity. So we all Shiv Sainiks [*sic*] will hold demonstrations clad in undergarments and go to each and every function where he is present."[36] It was no accident that the Shiv Sena targeted Dilip Kumar.[37] The former matinee idol had long been their *bête noir*. When the government of Pakistan had given Dilip Kumar their highest civil award, the Nishan-e-Pakistan, for his contribution to cinema, Shiv Sena had branded him a traitor.

By targeting Dilip Kumar, the Shiv Sena hoped to imply that *Fire* was an anti-Hindu conspiracy hatched by Muslims. Describing the film as an exercise in "Hindu bashing," Bal Thackeray asked: "Why should the film revolve around a Hindu family? Why has the filmmaker named the characters

---

36. Shiv Sainiks strip to tease Dilip Kumar over *Fire*, *Hindustan Times*, December 13, 1998.

37. Kumar (b. 1922) is considered one of Indian cinema's greatest actors. He began his acting career in 1944 and starred in a series of popular films in the 1940s, '50s, and '60s. Kumar has a huge fan following across South Asia and holds the record for winning the most number of Filmfare Best Actor Awards India's equivalent to the Oscars. Born in a Muslim family as Yusuf Khan, he chose the screen name Dilip Kumar believing it was advantageous to have Hindu name. In 1994, he was awarded the Dadasaheb Phalke Award (India's highest award for achievement in cinema).

Sita and Radha? Could not the filmmaker have named them Shabana, Saira, or Najma?" These names were jibes at Shabana Azmi and Dilip Kumar's actress wife Saira Bano. Thackeray asked: "Has lesbianism spread like an epidemic that it should be portrayed as a guideline to unhappy wives not to depend on their husbands and is this the meaning and message to be given to spoil younger generations and those who have no idea about it?" (ibid). In a strongly worded op-ed piece in the *Times of India*, Shabana Azmi warned that in targeting Dilip Kumar and communalizing the issue, the Shiv Sena was trying to deflect attention from the core issue of freedom of speech and expression. She said that by calling Dilip Kumar a traitor, Thackeray had insinuated that "a true Muslim cannot be a true Indian," thereby hurting the sentiments of "not only scores of Muslims in this country but also every citizen of India" (Azmi 1998).

The "underwear demonstration" came in for sharp criticism from all quarters, including leaders of the Hindu Right. BJP leader L.K. Advani expressed his displeasure by stating that while "peaceful demonstrations" were perfectly acceptable in a democracy, "violence, vandalism, or the display of "human [body] parts" was not acceptable.[38] The report also stated that the Prime Minister Atal Behari Vajpayee, senior most leader of the BJP, personally called up Dilip Kumar to express his regrets. On December 14, the Supreme Court

---

38. Advani slams Sena's strip Act', *The Hindustan Times*, December 14, 1998.

ordered the Central and State Governments of Maharashtra to provide full security to the petitioners who had appealed to the court for protection.

The Parliament was also in an uproar over the underwear demonstration. MP Ramdeo Bhandari condemned the Shiv Sena for insulting a "secular and nationalist" person like Dilip Kumar (*The Statesman*, December 15, 1998). The controversial Shiv Sena MP Sanjay Nirupam vociferously disagreed and insisted on characterizing the actor as a "traitor" and a "Pakistani." The remark drew loud protests from the dissenting parties who by now had now risen to their feet in protest. The Chairman of the Rajya Sabha (the upper house of Parliament) demanded an apology from Nirupam, as his "offensive comment" had brought disrepute to the House, Parliament, and the country. An unrepentant Nirupam refused. There was such pandemonium that the session had to be adjourned. On the same day, the Maharashtra Assembly was rocked by the same debate (ibid).

That evening, artists, writers, left-wing politicians, and citizens staged a candlelight vigil in New Delhi to protest against the attacks on Dilip Kumar. The protestors gathered outside the residence of home minister L.K. Advani and demanded that cultural policing by Shiv Sena be stopped. In its editorial titled 'Shameful antics' on December 15, 1998, the *Hindustan Times* lamented the "unfortunate lumpenization of political culture" in Bombay, a city whose reputation was being "so recklessly tarnished by an organization whose unfitness to be in the seat of power is becoming clearer by the day" (ibid).

By February 12, the Censor Board cleared *Fire* for public viewing once again without a single cut and announced that it would shortly be re-released for public viewing. Two weeks later, a re-certified *Fire* was released all across the country. In Delhi, both English and Hindi versions of the film were released without any cuts. In Bombay, the film was released, but the names of the two protagonists were dropped altogether. Describing the decision as "ridiculous," the lead editorial in the *Hindustan Times* remarked that it was "indeed weird" that, unlike in the rest of the country, Bombay audiences would see a film in which the two main characters had no names.[39]

If the Hindu Right's protests against *Fire* were aimed at discouraging people from watching the film, it certainly had the opposite effect. The film ran to packed houses in both northern and southern states, and in many places tickets were available only on the black market. Even though some screenings were accompanied by cat-calls, whistling, and hoots, *The Hindu* reported that women were turning out in large numbers to watch the film.[40] Women-only screenings witnessed long queues of female patrons. C.M. Naim de-

39. *Hindustan Times*, February 26, 1998.

40. *Fire* goes up in smoke, *The Hindu*, December 13, 1998.

scribed his experiences of watching the film in Lucknow, recalling that while "a great many men in the audience found much sexual excitement and voyeuristic pleasure in the film … at the same time I heard no comment … that could be called a denunciation of the film. It was clear that a good time had been had by all, that everyone's expectations had been met well" (Naim 1999). Notwithstanding the diverse audience responses, *Fire* recorded an eighty-percent collection from ticket sales at the box office.

The re-release of *Fire* marked a major victory for those who had opposed the politics of the Hindu Right and stood for freedom of speech and expression. At the end of the day, secular and progressive forces prevailed. Shabana Azmi summed up the mood of the people aptly when she wrote:

> There were spontaneous protests by not only women's organizations, film bodies and cultural organizations but by diverse groups ranging from housing rights activists, health care workers, academics, students, journalist and members of the audience. There are hundreds of letters to the editors and on the internet everyday condemning the Shiv Sena's attempt to establish might over right. The media has stood up in one voice for the right of freedom of expression and against the Shiv Sena's cultural dictatorship. The question is not whether *Fire* is a good film or a bad film. The question is who

will decide this. The people or the Shiv Sena? (Azmi 1998)

With the film no longer under a cloud of censorship, the many issues raised by the film could bear more thoughtful reflection.

TWO: YOU CAN SEE WITHOUT LOOKING

"Let the flames be my witness"

The camera moves through yellow flowers as a woman and a little girl walk through lush mustard fields. A family has come for a picnic and the mother tells her little girl a story. There were once a people who lived on a hill, and they were sad because they could never see the ocean. An old woman in the village comforts them. "What you can't see, you can see," she says. "You just have to see without looking." The mother asks the little girl, "Do you know what it means, Radha?" The girl doesn't. The mother laughs and hugs her and the screen fades to black.

The camera tilts down from black to reveal a young couple in silhouette leaning against the wall to face each other. They are framed against a square stone doorway opening into red stone arches. The woman walks away and sits down on the steps in front of the arches. The camera crosses over to hold the woman, Sita (Nandita Das), in a frontal shot. She's dressed in a bright orange sari; her bangles indicate that she has just been married. She looks thoughtful, perhaps even sad. The camera returns to the man in silhouette before moving away to pan through dark stone interiors and settle upon a square opening through which can be seen the Taj Mahal. The couple is in Agra, a common honeymoon

FIGURE 4. Sita and Jatin on their honeymoon at the Taj Mahal in Agra. DVD still.

destination. Sita walks into the frame and stops to contemplate the monument. A bird flies across the sky.

A tourist guide holds his audience enthralled with the story of Emperor Shah Jahan, who built the Taj Mahal as a memorial to his beloved wife Mumtaz Mahal. As Sita listens with interest, she is keenly aware that her new husband, Jatin (Jaaved Jaaferi), is not very interested. When she excitedly tells him that her favorite film *Taj Mahal* was shot here, Jatin looks bored. He does not like romantic films. When she asks what he likes, he mumbles, "Kung fu ... Bruce Lee, Jackie Chan ... from Hong Kong." The tourist guide continues his story about the "symbol of eternal love." Shah Jahan, he says, wanted to cut off the hands of his architect so that he could never design another Taj Mahal. In retaliation, the architect drilled a hole on the roof of the Taj so that the masterpiece would forever be flawed. As the crowd follows the guide toward the monument, which has now acquired a dark undertone, Sita asks Jatin, "Don't you like me?" He meets her eyes with difficulty and says, "Look, we've only been married for three days."

The next sequence establishes the Kapur household and the apartment where Sita will now live. On returning from their honeymoon, the newlyweds are welcomed into the family by Jatin's elder brother Ashok (Kulbhushan Kharbanda), his wife Radha (Shabana Azmi), his mute and paralytic mother, Biji (Kushal Rekhi), and the live-in houseboy, Mundu (Ranjit Chowdhry). Assisted by Mundu, Radha performs the auspicious rituals. Sita and Jatin touch the feet of the elders to seek their blessings after which the new bride is introduced to the frail and ailing mother-in-law. Mundu helpfully explains that since Biji has been the "victim of a major stroke," she does "no talking but much listening." Ashok takes a family photograph while mumbling something about Biji finally getting to see "a baby boy." The irrepressible Mundu announces his plan to go to Agra for his own honeymoon. Jatin rudely suggests that he visit the other famous destination in Agra—the lunatic asylum! Claiming that that he has an appointment with the "kung-fu video wholesalers," Jatin rushes out of the house. Ashok also leaves the room after remarking that "All good things must come to an end—back to work." After the men leave, Radha escorts Sita to Jatin's room. Nuttgen's camerawork washes the apartment with burn-outs and white highlights that envelop the characters in a dreamy soft light.

Sita enters Jatin's room to find that the walls are bare except for a few posters of Bruce Lee and Jackie Chan. Production designer Aradhana Seth recalls that she wanted to suggest that Jatin used his room like a hotel, returning there only to sleep because he spent most of his time between the video rental shop and his girlfriend's beauty salon. When Sita sits on the double bed in the middle of the room, the top-angle shot shows rose petals strewn across the bed. This was most likely a thoughtful gesture from Radha anticipating the couple's first night in the house. Sita opens the cupboard and surveys the contents. Something catches her fancy and she pulls it out—it's a pair of trousers. Having checked to ensure that no one is watching, she shuts the door and puts the trousers on under her thick, silk sari. She pulls her sari off and studies herself in the mirror. She's dressed in Jatin's oversized pants, a blouse that now looks like a short top, and her gold jewelry. Watching herself in the mirror, she unties her long hair with slow deliberation and lets it cascade around her shoulders. Then, lighting up a mock cigarette, she turns on a sexy Indi pop number and starts performing a vampish dance in front of the mirror. The performance is interrupted by urgent knocking on the bedroom door. Radha is standing outside trying not to look shocked at Sita's strange attire and the loud music. "Biji has been ringing her

FIGURE 5. The new bride at the Kapur household amuses herself with an impromptu performance. DVD still.

bell!" she says without expression. An apologetic Sita runs to her mother-in-law only to discover that Radha already attended to her. But Biji keeps ringing the bell; Radha explains that she's upset with Sita's "outfit." Sita looks mortified. How had she—a new bride—managed to appear before Biji dressed like this? She runs back into the bedroom, takes out a sari, and walks over to the dressing table when, on an impulse, she tosses the sari aside. Pulling down the blouse to reveal a bare shoulder, she strikes a seductive pose in front of the mirror and bursts out laughing. The mortification about her sartorial transgression has clearly not lasted long.

The subsequent sequences feature Julie (Alice Poon), Jatin's Chinese girlfriend, and Swamiji (Ram Gopal Bajaj), Ashok's guru and object of devotion. Julie, a hairdresser in

FIGURE 6. Jatin paints Julie's nails at the Darling Beauty Parlour. DVD still.

the Darling Beauty Parlor, declares, "If I have to blow-dry the hair of another fat cow, I swear I'll puke." When the lovers are first shown on screen, a subdued and vulnerable Jatin is painting Julie's toenails. He responds to her statement by commenting that had she married him, someone would have been doing *her* hair. "Silly boy," exclaims Julie, appearing for the first time in close-up, "do you know what the word "hunt' means?" As Jatin listens apprehensively, she continues: "It's my favorite word. It means to pursue, to chase for a game or kill. When we stop hunting all excitement fizzles out. You don't want that to happen to us, do you?" Jatin shakes his head and asks, "But at what cost?" Julie replies, "At all costs." "I can't live without you," says Jatin, kissing her feet tenderly. There is little doubt who the hunter is in this relationship.

FIGURE 7. At the ashram, Swamiji delivers a sermon on the dangers of desire. DVD still.

The next shot cuts to show Ashok clasping Swamiji's feet as he pays obeisance. Swamiji delivers a sermon at his ashram about the differences between "Desire Night" which is the "love of power" and "Aspiration Light" which is the "power of love." He asks his disciples how Desire Night might be expelled. His faithful disciple Ashok volunteers an answer: "Keep the objects of your temptation around you, and test yourself against them till all temptations and desires leave you. Because desire is the root of all evil." The two sequences sum up the obsessions of the two brothers. "One embraces celibacy, the other, a mistress" (Sengupta 2009, 100–18).

As Sita settles into the Kapur household, she makes several discoveries. She finds out that her husband is "occupied

FIGURE 8. Mundu masturbates to a porn flick as Biji (off-screen) watches helplessly. DVD still.

elsewhere" when Jatin carelessly leaves his wallet around with a photo of Julie in it. She also learns why Ashok keeps mentioning a "baby boy" in her presence when Radha tells her that she could not bear him a child. "So sorry, Madam, no eggs in ovaries" was what the doctor told her. Sita declares Ashok a "saint" after comparing him to a man back home who, in order to have a son, married three times and finally drove his first wife to kill herself. Radha has no option but to agree.

At this point, the audience also makes a discovery. Whenever Mundu is entrusted with the job of taking Biji upstairs to show her a video of the *Ramayana*, he plays one of Jatin's bootlegged porn videos and masturbates vigorously while the old lady flails her hand and groans helplessly. The sequence elicits both laughter and discomfort in the audience. Unable to protest, the mute woman can only moan loudly. Her loud, disapproving noises could well be mistaken for sounds of orgiastic pleasure except that Mundu has to bark at her to shut up. One day he nearly gets caught. Sita enters the room just as Mundu manages to pull up his pajamas and switch the videos. The sex sounds of the porn video are now replaced with the drone of sonorous dialogues from *Ramayana*. Sita is startled to find an emotionally distressed Biji and a profusely sweating Mundu. When she asks Mundu why Biji is so upset, he explains piously that every time Biji watches Sita's trial by fire, she cries because the scene is so emotional. In a moment of comic irony, Mundu dramatically starts spouting Sita's lines: "Let the flames be my witness. If I am impure, then the flames will destroy me, but if I am not, they will not touch me." The mythical Sita's trial by fire is a recurring motif in the film.

The Kapurs' terrace is a space of both work and leisure. Here the women hang clothes to dry while catching glimpses of the world outside. When Radha and Sita meet on the terrace for the first time, the busy neighborhood seems to be winding down. The night lights and bright neon signs frame the mise-en-scène as Sita looks at the city below. She hopes that Jatin will come home early. She tells Radha, "I've seen Delhi, I've also seen the Taj Mahal ... maybe next, Bombay." Then, as an afterthought, she adds, "Maybe, I'll run away ..." "To join the movies?" asks Radha indulgently. Sita replies, "Oh no. I just want to see the ocean." The camera holds Radha in a frontal mid-shot; she looks at Sita in wonderment as though a secret transaction has been made. "I too wanted to see the ocean once, but ..." says Radha without finishing the sentence. Ashok is heard calling out for her and she turns to go. Before moving out of the frame, she pauses to turn back. Framed against a burning highlight, Radha gives Sita a lingering look.

The next day, Jatin comes out of the shower to see Ashok sitting on his bed. An altercation follows which bears quoting in full:

Ashok: "Jatin, are you still seeing Julie?"

Jatin: "Yes ... [pulling a T-shirt over his head] Yes, I am ... I love her."

Ashok: "We told you we had no objection to you marrying a Chinese girl, but you said 'no to Julie and yes to Sita. Now, what's happening?"

Jatin: "What the hell do you mean, Bhai [brother]? It's Julie who said no to me! It's she who did not want to get stuck in a joint family and become a baby-making machine or something ... And as far as saying yes to Sita is concerned, you're forgetting that you and Biji made my life bloody hell. [He gets angrier,

and raises his voice.] Nagging, nagging. 'Jatin, you must get married, Jatin, you must have children."
[He turns to Ashok, who looks down apologetically.] What could I do? Did I have a choice? Living in a joint family, having a joint account … joint … [Ashok gets up to calm Jatin down. He places his hand on Jatin's chest and asks him to breathe deeply. Jatin looks at Ashok as if he's mad, then slumps down on the bed and continues to speak.] What did you think? A miracle would happen when I got married? That I would put Julie in my back-pocket and start loving Sita? And why feel sorry only for Sita? It's not easy, Bhai, being a yo-yo between what I want and what I am expected to want."

Ashok: "I am sorry, Jatin, but miracles do happen … [Ashok is now framed with a poster of Jackie Chan on the wall. Even Jackie Chan seems to look at Ashok with surprise.] You must give a chance to Sita. Your duty as husband demands that you do."

Jatin: "Duty? [Jatin stares at Ashok in anger and disbelief. The word has touched a raw nerve in Jatin. He speaks slowly and deliberately.] And what about your duty, Bhai? Huh? Everything you do is for that bloody Swamiji of yours."

Ashok delivers a stinging slap to Jatin's face and storms

out of the room. Radha follows him into their bedroom. (Perhaps it was Radha who had encouraged Ashok to have a talk with his brother, hoping that it would help Sita.) A defeated Ashok sits on the bed while his wife places a comforting hand on his shoulder. He is despondent not because he has hit his brother but because he has lost control over his emotions. He removes Radha's consoling hand from his shoulder so that all desires are kept at bay. As if in reply to Jatin's allegations, he tells Radha, "You must forgive me. My choices have made life difficult for you."[41]

This conversation between Ashok and Jatin is one of the moments in the film when the husbands are granted an empathetic subjectivity. The pressures of compulsory marriage impact deleteriously on men even as the system privileges the upper-caste, heteronormative man. However, unlike the women, who have to choose between desire and duty, the men are able to lay claim to both. Ashok and Jatin take their wives for granted while they pursue their respective objects of desire. Later, when Radha asks Ashok how his vow of abstinence is likely to help her, he thinks for some time before replying that it is the duty of the wife to help her husband.[42]

41. In the Hindi version of the film, Ashok asks, "Will you ever be able to forgive me?" By turning the statement into a question, Ashok is allowed to express doubt and uncertainty, which gives his character a greater complexity, perhaps, than in the English version.

42. Ashok takes his time responding to Radha's question. Finally,

This scene also highlights one of the cinematic weaknesses of the film, its use of excessive and unwieldy dialogue. That the dialogue is spoken in English aggravates the problem. It is unlikely that a middle-class Punjabi family living in Lajpat Nagar would carry out their daily conversations in English. It is equally absurd that Mundu, given his caste and class status, should converse with his employers in fluent English. For a film that uses realism as a narrative strategy, the choice of language impedes the flow of the film. Apart from asking the audience to suspend certain expectations of realism, the use of English by all the characters in the film disallows any reference to social categories (Naim 1999). In India, language and its deployment are heavily inscribed by caste and class privileges. For this reason, the Hindi version of the film not only works better for South Asian audiences but considerably improves the performance of the actors.[43]

Perhaps in response to his brother's exhortations about husbandly duties, Jatin has rough, perfunctory sex with Sita that night, leaving her hurt and bleeding. Despite Jatin's casual assurance that "it happens the first time," Sita is

---

when he does reply, he is barely able to meet her eyes. Kulbhushan Kharband's excellent performance seems to convey Ashok's own doubts about the soundness of his own argument.

43. The incongruity did not escape Mehta, but had she subtitled the film, it would have been marketed as a foreign film in the English-speaking world.

unnerved by the experience. As he sleeps peacefully, she tries to scrub the blood stains away. In the next bedroom, Ashok has been testing himself against the object of his temptation, Radha.[44] Experiment over, she returns to her own bed where, framed by the mosquito net, she stares off-screen. The mustard fields reappear. Radha sits on her mother's lap among the lush reeds while her father looks on. "When, Ma?" she asks. "Soon," her mother replies. The promise keeps Radha going.

Radha is introduced as Biji's caregiver. In a mise-en-scène bathed in white highlights, Radha gets Biji dressed and ready for the arrival of the newlyweds. The old woman smiles fondly when Radha covers her head with a *dupatta* and hands her the small metal bell to summon help. Radha goes down to the food takeout area and instructs Mundu to give Biji her milk. In the Hindi version, Radha hums a song as she runs from one errand to another. This additional stage business (which is absent from the English version) allows her to claim a cheerfulness that displaces any singular reading of her as monotonously unhappy member of the Kapur household.

When Sita and Radha meet on the terrace again, a wedding procession is winding its way through the street below.

---

44. In *Fire*, Ashok's method of overcoming temptation by using his wife is a jibe at Gandhi, who tested his own strength by using women close to him.

FIGURE 9. Radha and Sita kiss for the first time. DVD still.

"Again, someone is getting married," says Sita. Radha keeps looking at Sita when she says, "Yes, again." Their eyes linger on each other as they speak. In the next scene, Radha enters Sita's room to find that she's sitting on the bed crying. "I want to go back home," says Sita. Radha takes her in her arms and comforts her like a child. "Don't worry," she says. "Things will work out with Jatin." A sobbing Sita replies, "It's not *that* ..." Radha draws back as they continue to look at each other. Sita clasps Radha by the neck, pulls her toward herself, and kisses her on the lips. Radha does not resist, but then gently extricates herself and leaves the room.

Radha stares at herself in the bathroom mirror. She has left the tap running in the basin. Very slowly she raises her hand to touch her lips. The mustard fields appear, once again. "Why is mother crying?" little Radha asks her father.

"Because she is happy," he replies. "Can't you see what the fields have become?" asks the mother. Radha still cannot. Her mother tells her not to look so hard but close her eyes and see. Radha tries but fails. Read together with the preceding sequence, one could ask whether Sita was also crying out of happiness. Had she caught a glimpse of the ocean and seen the fields transform? Had she been begun to see without looking?

"*Sita, Madam, is too modern*"

Radha is unsettled by their first kiss. At night she reaches out for Ashok, who turns away. The next morning, lost in thought, she stares into the sun-drenched light outside the window. Hearing someone enter the room, she turns, and as her eyes adjust to the darkness inside the house, she sees Sita standing behind her. "Will you oil my hair?" Sita asks Radha. In one of the most lyrical sequences in the films, Radha stands over Sita gently massaging the oil into her hair. The women exchange glances as they stand, framed and shot through a full length dressing-table mirror. As Radha looks up, she meets Sita's adoring gaze. She is shy but not afraid to return the gaze. Any discomfort she may have felt seems to have melted away.

The next day is the North Indian Hindu festival of Karva Chauth. On this day, a dutiful Radha and a reluctant Sita will fast for the long life of their husbands. According to custom, the fast is broken after the wives sight the moon

FIGURE 10. The women steal glances as Radha oils Sita's hair. DVD still.

and get the blessings of their husbands. Feminists have had a longstanding critique of this ritual because it perpetuates myths around male supremacy and female subordination while glorifying regressive notions of *pati parmeshwar* or the idea that the husband is god.[45] When Sita wakes up at dawn, she finds that Radha and Mundu have laid out an elaborate spread on the table. As they sit down to eat, the women have the following conversation:

Sita: "I think I'll just have some tea."

45. In the 1990s, blockbuster films such as *Dilwale Dulhaniya Le Jayenge* (*The Lover Gets the Bride*, Aditya Chopra, 1995) revived and spectacularized the celebration of Karva Chauth in popular Bombay cinema.

Radha: "You might regret not eating, later."

Sita: "So … what do we have to do today?"

Radha: "Wear fancy saris, heavy jewelry … anything we wish."

Sita: "Except eat and drink."

Radha: [smiling indulgently] "You don't have to keep the fast if you don't want."

Sita: "You must be joking. My mother would kill me. And Biji … she'll never stop ringing the bell. [Radha looks down.] Isn't it amazing, how we are bound by customs and rituals? [Radha looks at Sita and listens attentively.] Someone just has to press my button— this button marked tradition—and I start responding like a trained monkey." [Sita looks up to find Radha gazing at her.] "Do I shock you?"

Radha: "Yes."

[Sita comes around the table and puts her arms around Radha who smiles and reaches up to clasp her hand.]

Sita: "You are lovely."

Jatin tells Sita that since he doesn't believe in these rituals, she shouldn't fast for him. Sita says she has no choice in the matter. "Then go right ahead," replies Jatin. Ashok, on the other hand, is pleased that Radha is fasting for him. With Swamiji's framed photograph standing over the separation of their beds, Ashok smears the *sindoor* (red vermillion) in the parting of her hair. As Radha touches Ashok's feet, he asks: "Are you happy?" then adds benevolently, "Take it easy. Fasting without water was difficult even for Mahatma Gandhi." If nothing else, Karva Chauth breaks the tedium of everyday household chores. With Jatin and Ashok out of the house, the rest of the family has gathered in the living room. As the day goes by, Mundu and Biji keep a check to see that the women are indeed fasting. Biji rings her bell each time Sita makes an irreverent comment. Radha decides to enlighten Sita about the ritual by recounting the legend of Karva Chauth, the story of a queen's devotion to her royal husband and her final reward and salvation: There lived a king who was so handsome and wealthy that even the gods envied him. But as he was also arrogant, the gods decided to punish him. So one day, the king was felled by hundreds of needles impaled in his body. His devoted and loyal wife spent one whole year plucking out the needles, one by one. When there were only two left to be pulled out—one over each eye—a holy man suddenly appeared and demanded the queen's attention. The wily maid seized the opportunity to pull out the two remaining needles, bringing the king back to life. When the king opened his eyes, he believed he had been saved by the devotion of the maid, so he made her his queen and turned the real queen into a maid. The holy man, who witnessed everything, advised the queen to undertake a fast without food or water from dawn to moonrise, after which the spell would be broken. The queen kept the fast, and the spell was, indeed, broken. The king reinstated his rightful queen and cast the deceitful maid away.

Radha's narration of the story is transformed into kitschy visual narrative by Mundu's colorful imagination. Staged through the aesthetics of calendar art and the cinematic genre of mythologicals, the enactment of the Karva Chauth story allows Mundu a rare moment of subjectivity. In his imagined narrative, he is king and Radha is his queen, thereby revealing, for the first time, his erotic attraction to her. Predictably, Ashok is the holy man, while Mundu's "hero," Jatin, is reduced to a lowly attendant. Sita, his rival in real life, is the devious maid who is suitably punished in the end. Performed with the exaggerated theatricality of a sloppy amateur play, Mundu's narrative has a wish-fulfilling closure: he is united with the woman of his dreams—Radha. That Mundu's fantasyscape should be rendered through the matrix of televisual kitsch underscores the irony of the unsettled domestic situation and foreshadows the sexual transgressions that are about to follow.

The close shots now reveal a subtle change in Radha. She is brighter and happier and seems to have started to take a new interest in her appearance. The red *bindi* on her forehead and

FIGURE 11. "The queen didn't have many choices," says Radha as Mundu looks on. She's falling in love with Sita. DVD still.

the kohl around her eyes make her look brighter and definitely happier. In a room with four people, the two women look only at each other. Sita is not impressed with the moral of the Karva Chauth story, and she wonders aloud why the queen does not leave the king. Mundu is horrified. "No, no," he protests. "Once you are married, you are stuck together like glue." Sita looks into Radha's eyes and asks, "What do *you* think?" Radha gazes back at her and tentatively replies, "I don't know … She did not have many choices." "I am so sick of all this devotion!" says Sita in exasperation. Then, looking at Radha, she says, "I am sure we can find choices." The sentence is completed over a lingering close-up of Radha, who looks intently at the woman with whom she is falling in love. Sita's unconventional comments hold a tremulous attraction

FIGURE 12. Radha takes Jatin's place and breaks Sita's fast for Karva Chauth. DVD still.

for her. But Biji rings the bell furiously at Sita's words while Mundu concludes that, "Sita, Madam, is too modern."

When the moon rises in the evening, Radha and Sita complete the rituals of Karva Chauth on the terrace. They see the moon, but Sita is unable to break her fast because Jatin is not at home to bless her. Radha breaks custom by offering Sita a glass of water, substituting Jatin's blessings with her own. Sita drinks the water and breaks her fast. As they look at each other, the implications of reworking the ritual do not escape them. The ritual of Karva Chauth is subverted and reconstituted, rendered meaningless and infused with new meaning. Disobedience becomes both an oppositional discourse and the language of reclamation.

That night, Sita is unable to fall asleep. She sits up in bed

FIGURE 13. Radha and Sita make love for the first time. DVD still.

and, to the sound of A.R. Rahman's haunting soundtrack, runs her fingers over her lips. The next shot is taken from inside Radha's room. The door opens and Sita enters. The camera moves behind the gauzy mosquito net as she approaches Radha's bed. Lifting the net, she climbs onto the bed and lies down next to Radha, whose back is turned towards her. She places her hand tenderly on Radha's shoulder. "Go back to your room," she tells Sita, who instead begins to caress her. Radha reciprocates, and they kiss. Radha turns toward Sita and takes her in her arms. The next shot is taken from a distance and through the mosquito net, so that only their silhouettes can be seen as the women make love to each other.

This is the first explicit sequence of lesbian love-making

in any film in India. Nandita Das has recalled that, initially, this was a particularly difficult sequence for her to do. She had never made love to a woman and was not able to get it quite right. They worked on the scene until Mehta was satisfied with the take. Das has said that the awkwardness melted away as the film progressed and she became closer to Azmi. The intimacy they developed helped them become comfortable with each other's bodies. In retrospect, Das believes that the slight awkwardness of the first love-making scene fits the sequence well, because it approximated the experience of the screen characters, who were also having lesbian sex for the first time.

Here, I would like to digress slightly and draw attention to an unintended allusion to a Bengali film, *Streer Patra* (*Letter from the Wife*, 1976), directed by Purnendu Pattrea. Based on a short story of the same name by the famous Bengali writer Rabindranath Tagore, *Streer Patra* is about a married woman's resistance to the dictates of conventional society that culminates in her leaving her marriage in search of a world larger than her marriage and family. Mrinalini, the central protagonist and author of the letter, is driven to confront the oppressive condition of her married life when Bindu, a younger woman, takes shelter in her house. She mentors and nurtures Bindu, whom the rest of the household treats with cruelty. At the end of the story, when Bindu is driven to suicide, Mrinalini decides to never return to her husband's home. The short story is her valedictory letter to her husband. Describing her relationship to Bindu, she writes:

> When Bindu lost her fear of me, she tied herself in
> yet another knot. She developed so a great a love for
> me that it made me afraid. I have never seen such an
> image of love in my household. I have read of such
> love in books but that was love between men and
> women. For a long time there had been no occasion
> for me to recall that I was beautiful—now, after so
> many years, this ugly girl became obsessed with my
> beauty. It was as if her eyes could never have enough
> of gazing on my face.

The film invokes female homoeroticism through a strategy of indirection and an invitation to read it intertextually with Tagore's short story. Historian Tanika Sarkar suggests that *Streer Patra* might frustrate the contemporary feminist reader because neither Mrinalini nor Bindu fight for sexual freedom, and there are no explicit references made to their sexual lives—although there is an unmistakable suggestion of eroticism in the story. She writes: "A most revolutionary desire has been suggested by Tagore, rather clearly. It is through the eyes of Bindu that Mrinalini first begins to realize that she is beautiful" (Sarkar 2001, 35–46). In a sequence that echoes the one discussed above, Mrinalini nurses an ailing Bindu as they lie together in bed. Before the sequence fades to black, Mrinalini asks Bindu to turn toward her and come into her embrace. At the start of the new millennium, an architecturally similar composition appeared in a more explicit television film about lesbian desire titled *Ushno Taar Jonno* (*Warm for Her/For the Sake of Warmth*, Kaushik Ganguly, 2002). Here again, one woman nurses the other as they lie in bed, but in the more recent sequence, the embrace is completed and sealed with a kiss.[46]

After their first love-making, Radha gets off the bed and wears the *salwar* lying on the floor. This particular shot has been derided as crude by several commentators, but by making the sexuality explicit, Mehta extricates the relationship from the ambiguous gestures of female homosocial intimacy. Sita still lies in bed covered by a sheet that leaves her shoulders bare. She asks Radha, "Did we do anything wrong?" Radha sits down on the bed next to her, looks into Sita's eyes, and says, "No." Sita kisses her hand in gratitude. The camera returns to the living room to watch Sita emerge from inside Radha's bedroom. As she walks back to her own room, she stops against a window to button her blouse. In the darkness of the living room, Biji, now awake, silently watches her.

The next day, a disapproving Mundu espies a private ritual. As he dusts the videotapes in Jatin's library, he surveys the two women in the takeout kitchen. Radha has bought glass bangles for Sita and, from Mundu's point of view, we

46. The episode was part of the series titled *Stories of Domesticity*, telecast on ETV Bangla.

FIGURE 14. Radha and Sita adorn each other's wrists with bangles and create their own ritual of love. DVD still.

witness the two women place them on each other's wrists. The music track underscores this moment of intimate transaction. Bonded by their love, Radha and Sita become complicit in transforming mundane chores into pleasurable activities. Mundu concludes: "Even Radha Bhaabi [sister-in-law] looks like a heroine. Now there are two heroines in one kitchen." The two sequences described above develop the parallel tracks of love and danger. As Radha and Sita become increasingly involved, they move that much closer to being found out. For the audience, both Biji and Mundu carry the threat of disclosure; they are witnesses in whose presence the relationship starts to unfold.

Homosocial activities—gestures of friendship and duty—provide cover to Radha and Sita's sexual involvement. This

FIGURE 15. Sita dutifully massages Radha's feet at the family picnic in Lodhi Gardens. DVD still.

idea plays most elegantly when the family goes for a picnic to Delhi's Lodi Gardens. Having finished their lunch, Ashok suggests that Jatin and Sita go for a walk, but Jatin decides to lie down instead. Sita makes a proposition to Radha: "Since you've been cooking all morning, let me massage your feet." An embarrassed Radha protests, but Jatin says, "Yes, Sita, do that. Give dear Bhaabi a good massage." Sita dutifully agrees and gently pulls Radha's feet onto her lap. The camera pauses to hold Sita's hands softly massaging Radha's feet, then tilts up to show her in close-up as she smiles disarmingly. In South Asia, elders often have their feet massaged by younger members of the family, and it is therefore perfectly natural that the younger daughter-in-law should attend to her elder counterpart in this fashion. The queer viewing pleasure of this sequence lies in understanding that Sita's ready compliance does not spring from familial obligation or a sense of duty. The camera now moves to Radha, whose expression changes from being awkward and embarrassed to being amused and pleasured at the same time. Biji and Jatin sleep peacefully, while Sita earnestly massages Radha's feet. Ashok surveys his family and, pleased by what he sees, declares: "I am lucky to have such a good family." Sita can barely stifle a laugh.

"Too much electricity"

Radha is surprised at her own transformation. The gradual excavation of erotic desire teaches Radha to disobey the dictates of Hindu middle-class traditions. She allows herself to be led astray by the disobedient Sita, whose first miscarriage of housewifely duties occurs on the day she arrives at the house, when she fails to hear Biji's bell. From Sita, Radha unlearns the compulsions of duty, traditional expectations, and compulsory heterosexuality. The relationship not only infuses their own lives with a new energy but shifts the balance of power within the family. This is powerfully expressed in one of the film's most cinematically accomplished sequences. It is dinner time at the Kapur household, and Nuttgens' camera moves effortlessly to capture the ensemble of characters in an overlapping choreography of actions. Radha cooks in the kitchen and Sita ferries hot food to the table where Ashok is eating. He asks his brother to come to the table before the food gets cold, but Jatin is busy yelling for Mundu because he can't find his Armani T-shirt. Meanwhile, Mundu is trying to feed Biji, who refuses to be fed by him, so Jatin turns around and loudly orders Sita to help him; like an obedient wife, she goes running into the bedroom. "Bhaabi, Biji won't eat," bleats Mundu, while Ashok mechanically repeats the line to Radha who, out of sheer habit, turns to walk towards Biji—then stops. Turning to face the camera and Ashok, she asks, "Why don't *you* feed Biji tonight?" This unexpected request stumps Ashok. He looks at her, looks at the food, and since the request doesn't seem unreasonable (she's *his* mother, after all), manages to say, "Of course." As Ashok exits the frame to go feed his mother, the camera holds Radha in a frontal shot. In a masterfully acted sequence, Shabana Azmi conveys a multitude of emotions—including amazement, triumph, fear, and relief—as she approaches the dining table and sits down on the chair that, until now, her husband had been occupying.

Meanwhile, Jatin and Sita emerge from their room. Ignoring the food on the table, Jatin prepares to walk out of the door. "You are not going anywhere" barks Ashok. "Why, Ashok Bhai?" snaps Jatin. "You go out morning noon and night to Swamiji's—why can't I go?" Biji looks on attentively as Ashok explains that he goes to Swamiji to "become a better person." Sita comes up behind Jatin and says, "Please, Ashok Bhaiya, let Jatin go. He has something important to do." Jatin turns to look at her in surprise: "Why are *you* so

keen that I go?" As Jatin leaves, Sita sits down at the table.
"It's not my fault she won't eat," says Mundu, bringing a
bowl of soup to Radha. "It's okay," says Radha comfortingly.
As the two women sit at the dining table in the foreground,
Nuttgens' effortlessly fluid camera frames Biji and Ashok in
the background. "Aren't you going to Swamiji's tonight?"
asks Radha eagerly. "As soon as Biji finishes her dinner," replies Ashok. The lovers are impatient to be left alone. That
is precisely what Biji dreads, so she starts ringing her bell
furiously. Ashok puts his arm around her affectionately and
says, "She doesn't want me to leave." The women look at
each other uneasily. Is it possible that Biji suspects? With
each passing day, love and danger come dangerously closer.

It has been argued that one of the reasons *Fire* became
so controversial was because it depicted lesbianism within
an ordinary household (Vanita and Kidwai 2001, 244–46).
Depictions of homosexuality in domestic situations—as in
Ismat Chugtai's short story "Lihaf" ("The quilt") and several
other instances—tended to be attacked more virulently than
the depiction of homosexuality in other same-sex environ-
ments. As long as homosexuality was seen to be occurring
in non-normative spaces, it could be seen as a "perversion
caused by an unfortunate situation than an active preference." But ironically, most homosexual or bisexual people in
India "are married at some time in their lives, live in the everyday world—in ordinary families, workplaces and neigh-
borhoods—and look indistinguishable from heterosexually

FIGURE 16. "Don't go ... please don't go," whispers Sita as Ashok calls out for Radha. DVD still.

inclined people" (ibid, 244). The power of *Fire* lies precisely in being able to evoke the specter of lesbian desire in a seemingly normative family.

Consequently, everyday spaces become inhabited by queer desires. In an evocatively lit sequence, Sita and Radha play hopscotch on the terrace. When Sita slips and loses her turn, she playfully begs Radha to give her another chance. As Radha kneels down to claim her turn, she notices a trickle of sweat running down Sita's legs. Radha catches a droplet on her fingertip, raises it to her lips, and licks it. In half-lit quasi silhouette, Sita kneels down, takes Radha's face in her hands and kisses her on the lips. Ashok's voice calling out for Radha cuts through the silence. "Don't go ... please don't go," whispers Sita. Radha kisses Sita's hand.

FIGURE 17. Radha looks at herself in the mirror as though she were rediscovering her own beauty. DVD still.

When Radha goes down to her bedroom, Ashok demands to know where she was. "With Sita," replies Radha, sitting down at the dressing table. The camera holds Radha in frontal close-up on the right of the frame as Ashok occupies the left in soft focus. In even softer focus on the right hand corner of the frame is a portrait of Swamiji. "Good," replies Ashok. "She looks happy these days. Maybe she is pregnant." Ashok's vow of celibacy does not seem to have diminished his obsession with procreation but what he does not see is that it is Radha who looks happy. The frame invites a closer look at Radha who, in turn, looks at herself in the mirror as though taking in her own beauty for the first time. Contemplating the changes in herself, she continues to answer Ashok's questions with a quiet determination that is new for her. "Did you not hear me calling?" asks Ashok. "Yes," she says. "Then why didn't you come?" he asks. As she removes her earrings for the night, Radha replies, "Sita says the concept of duty is overrated." That night Radha refuses to offer herself for her husband's test of will. She stretches out on her own bed, saying, "Not tonight, Ashok." In the next bedroom, Jatin jumps on Sita to perform his husbandly duties only to be pushed away. "You don't want?" he asks in disbelief. When she says no, he rolls over to sleep. Unknown to the husbands, a quiet rebellion has begun.

A key sequence unfolds next. The daughters-in-law put on a performance for Biji. To the accompaniment of a recorded love duet, the two women perform a song-and-dance routine like the ones in Bombay films.[47] Radha is the femme heroine while Sita, dressed in a grey suit, tie, and baseball cap, is the butch hero. As the women animatedly dance and lip-synch to the song, a delighted Biji looks on. The camera moves fluidly to capture the movements of the women, it catches a glimpse of Mundu's outline in soft-focus. He too is watching. A cross-dressed Sita playfully courts Radha through the song, and she reciprocates by miming the actions of a typical heroine. Then, as the song comes to an

---

47. Deepa Mehta excels in staging drag performances. In *Sam and Me*, Jaaferi dances in drag to a Bombay film song for the benefit of his male buddies and in *Bollywood/Hollywood*, Chowdhry plays Rockini, "the first drag queen from the land of *Kamasutra*." His drag performances are some of the best sequences in the film.

FIGURE 18. Sita dresses in drag to perform a Bombay film-style romantic love-duet with Radha as Biji and Mundu (off-screen) look on. DVD still.

end, Sita and Radha, in playful embrace, sink to the floor. As they disappear under the frame, we are left looking at Biji, whose expression of delight has changed to severe disapproval. As the last stanzas of the song plays out over Biji's troubled expression, one can only guess that the performers have crossed the line of play-acting. The extent of transgression can only be inferred by through the reaction of the onlookers. Mundu shakes his head from behind the curtain and concludes, "Too much electricity."

"*I desire to live again*"

Pleasure and danger collide unexpectedly when Radha catches Mundu masturbating to a porn video while Biji watches in distress. A shocked and furious Radha slaps Mundu and threatens to throw him out of the house. To avenge his humiliation, Mundu makes two disclosures. He reveals that the porn videos belong to Jatin who rents them out to "special customers" and "that hanky-panky between you and Sita, Madam, is not good for the family name." Mundu's words send a chill up Radha's spine. Biji has heard, and her worst fears are confirmed. She savagely pounds her metal bell on the bed.

From this moment on, the threat of being outed hangs precariously over the lovers. Despite Radha and Sita's insistence that Mundu should be fired, Ashok gives him a second chance. The women's inability to have him sacked only bolsters his cocky self-confidence. When he's alone with Radha in the kitchen, he sings an old Hindi film song: "Tell me, Radha, will our union take place?"[48] When the work day is over, Mundu seems preoccupied. He takes out a photograph from the inner pocket of his shirt and stares at it. It's the photograph that Ashok took when Sita first arrived in the house. With black ink, Mundu has crossed out everyone's faces except one. Radha's face has been circled with red ink—in the shape of a heart. That evening, Mundu spies on the two women through the keyhole and overhears their

48. Mundu sings a well-known song from the film *Sangam* (*Confluence*, Raj Kapoor, 1964) in which the heroine's name is also Radha. The song became a hit and was particularly relished for its naughty double entendre.

FIGURE 19. Through the crack in the door, Ashok (off-screen) watches his wife make love. DVD still.

conversation. He thinks about this for a while and then decides to go to the Ashram to inform Ashok.

As Ashok climbs the stairs to the bedroom, he suddenly turns around and tells Mundu to pack his bags. Mundu can't believe his ears. Why would he be punished for being loyal to his master? Mundu realizes only too late that class is a hard barrier to cross. "Bastard, he doesn't want me to watch his shame," mutters Mundu before abjectly begging to retain his job. In a stance typical of the Indian middle-class, Ashok threatens to hand him over to the police if he does not leave. The camera shows Mundu from behind as he sits down dejectedly on the staircase. This is the last we see of him.

The film now moves quickly toward its climax. Ashok opens the door slightly, peers through the crack, and watches his wife make love to her lover. Ashok barges into the bedroom and the soundtrack falls silent. It becomes imperative for the women to leave the house. Sita leaves first and tells Radha that she will wait for her at the Nizamuddin Shrine, while Radha stays back to have a last conversation with Ashok. Meanwhile, Ashok is haunted by the vision of his wife making love to her female lover. The images of Radha kissing Sita's hands and caressing her breast wrack him with rage and desire. Ashok's attempt to restore order in his house and marriage are clumsy. He tries to subdue Radha with intimidation, insults, awkward kisses, and dire warnings about desire bringing only ruin. At this point, Radha delivers the lines that the sequence has been building toward: "Without desire I was dead. Without desire there is no point in living … I desire Sita. I desire her warmth, her compassion, her body. I desire to live again." This is the culmination of Radha's journey. The woman who spoke in ungrammatical fragments—"No eggs in ovaries"—can now eloquently articulate her desire to desire.[49]

During this final confrontation, Radha's sari catches fire

---

49. Azmi considered her acting in this sequence to be one of her best performances in the film. She has said that delivering the rebellious lines with restraint was a challenge, but that it helped her that the cast and crew were preoccupied with safely executing the sequence of the sari catching fire. This distraction allowed her to escape attention and prepare for and deliver a powerful performance. (Interview with author on March 14, 2010.)

on the kitchen stove. This is the film's literal and metaphorical climax of *agni pariksha*, the trial by fire. In a conceptually and cinematically weak climactic sequence, Ashok—who has so far been portrayed with some complexity—metamorphoses into a villain when he leaves his wife to burn to death. Historically, fire deaths in India have claimed the lives of thousands of women whose brutal husbands and in-laws would set them on fire and later claim that they had died in kitchen-fire accidents, but there is nothing in the film to suggest that the Kapur family, least of all Ashok, is so inclined. A conservative family is not necessarily one that punishes its erring women with death.[50] Ashok's reaction to her transgression, which includes his being aroused, is as excessive as Radha's *agni pariksha* is contrived. As a result, the final sequences leading up to the happy dénouement at the *dargah* (shrine) appear hurried and cluttered.

When Radha's sari catches fire, Ashok watches dispassionately. Leaving Radha to wrestle with her fate, he picks up Biji and leaves the room. The sequence fades to white, after which the yellow flowers of the mustard fields reappear. This time, little Radha is on her own. Her eyes are shut, but

---

50. In *Heaven on Earth* (2008), Mehta created a family environment constantly charged with a seething undercurrent of violence. The lurking physical threat to Chand is painstakingly built throughout the film. This is not how Mehta develops the family environment in *Fire*, so at the end of the film, Ashok's indirect "attempt to murder" seems out of character.

FIGURE 20. As Radha's saree catches fire, Ashok (off-screen) does
nothing to help. DVD still.

she can finally see the ocean. Sita waits at the shrine as the
rain comes down in sheets. When Radha finally arrives, she
is bruised and her clothes are half-burnt. The film ends with
a high-angle shot of the two women embracing each other
as they, in turn, are embraced by the expansive architecture
of the shrine that now shelters their love.

Some viewers may wonder whether the "happy ending"
of *Fire* is to be understood literally or as a wish-fulfilling
fantasy. All film texts offer themselves to multiple readings,
so viewers are entitled to have their own interpretations.
How might we conclude that the sequence is not real but
phantasmatic? Mehta does not use any distinctive stylistic
trope to distinguish this sequence from the rest of the film,
nor does she, as in *Heaven on Earth*, confound the cinematic

FIGURE 21. The film ends as the lovers are reunited at the Nizamuddin shrine. DVD still.

borderlines of reality and fantasy. While several reviews in Canada and the US have described *Fire* as a "melodrama," Indian audiences are more likely to read the film as one that deploys the conventions of "realism" associated with the narrative strategies of regional and parallel cinema. The film scrupulously avoids the emotional excesses of Bollywood melodrama, including its most distinctive trope—the song-and-dance sequence—except as performance within performance. Yet *Fire* reveals important continuities with the conventions of Bollywood melodrama.[51] The plot, for example,

51. Mehta's films demonstrate a conflicted approach to Bombay cinema's melodramatic traditions and non-realist form. This is illustrated by a film like *Bollywood/Hollywood*, which is an elaborate spoof on those cinematic traditions.

can be seen as "ensconced in a Bollywood lineage—the trials and tribulations of difficult love" (Patel 2007, 222–33). The love between the two women is articulated through Bombay cinema's conventions of romantic love, including the eroticism of exchanged glances. The drag performances in Mehta's films—including the one in *Fire*—continue the Bollywood convention of using song-and-dance sequences for the play of forbidden love and transgressive desires. But most importantly, *Fire* pays tribute to Bombay cinema's enduring legacy of privileging romantic love over all other emotions. In this tradition, lovers are always united whether in love or death. Therefore, neither the tropes of realism nor the conventions of popular cinema that *Fire* deploys lead us to understand the happy ending as phantasmatic.

THREE: QUEER INCITEMENTS

Is it Canadian? Is it Indian? No, it's lesbian!
In discussing the reception and circulation of *Fire* in Canada and the US, Jigna Desai observes that most mainstream responses to the film betrayed an inability to locate the film as part of (Canadian) national cinema, identify its cinematic form and genre, or understand its gender and sexual politics to be contemporary (Desai 2002, 68–69). She argues that these "neocolonial responses suggest that South Asian (diasporic) cinema, politics and sexualities are read as part of an evolutionary process in which South Asia slowly follows the linear progress of the western nations in developing its national politics and cultures." A number of western critics, Desai wrote, "placed the film and it contents in a space marked as 'protofeminist' or 'pregay'" (ibid, 68).

Speculating about why the Indian censors had passed *Fire* without any cuts, Daniel Lak of *BBC Online* concluded that the decision of the Censor Board could signify either that *Fire* had been recognized as an important film or be "taken as an indication that [Indian] society remains ignorant or unaware of the sexual options before women" (Lak, 1998). In other words, backward India was lagging behind in the teleology of liberalism and had yet to wake up to women's sexual choices. Along similar lines, the *New York Times* stated:

"Perhaps bold and novel in India, its feminist messages seem dated by American standards" (Van Gelder 1996). A review in *Maclean's* lamented that *Fire*'s portrayal of "sexual transgression seems tame by Canadian standards."[52] *Time* magazine declared that the "Sapphic scenes would be incendiary for Indian audiences, discreet for Westerners."[53] Gayatri Gopinath has remarked that a number of critics used the film as an occasion to "replay colonial constructions of India as a site of regressive gender oppressions against which the West stands for enlightened egalitarianism" (Gopinath 2005). Leela Gandhi is correct to caution that "a politically careless imputation of a schism between homosexuality and Indian tradition only serves to nourish the hysterical and homophobic rhetoric of conservative lobbies [in India] eager to perpetuate the myth that same-sex love is a disease from the west" (Gandhi 2002, 87).

Despite the CBFC having cleared the film (not once but twice) for public viewing without cuts, the video of *Fire* continued to be marketed in the US and Canada as "Banned in India." Unable to see the opposition to *Fire* as part of a continuing cultural war, critics and commentators in North America rushed to present the conflict as one between tradition and modernity. This view can be seen to be a logical

52. Brian D. Johnson, Forbidden flames, *Maclean's*, September 29, 1997.

53. Cannes in Canada, *Time*, September 23, 1996.

extension of the persistent Eurocentric belief that history is a grand progressive narrative where the masses of the world march toward a singular civilizational future. While some (European) cultures were destined to arrive early, others had to remain in waiting. In the words of historian Dipesh Chakrabarty, this historicist argument consigned "Indians, Africans, and other 'rude' nations to an "imaginary waiting room of history," waiting their turn to be modern (Chakrabarty 2000, 8).

Gopinath suggests that, paradoxically, *Fire*'s narrative may have played a part in instigating this false polarity by framing the heroines' dilemma as one in which modernity, with its promise of individual freedom and self-expression, is pitted against tradition, which demands an adherence to prescribed roles as good Hindu wives. She writes: "The dichotomies through which the film is structured—between Biji and Sita, saris and jeans, silence and speech, self-denial and self-fulfillment, abstinence and desire, tradition and modernity—implicate it in a familiar teleological narrative of progress towards the individual 'freedom' offered by the West, against which the non-West can be read only as premodern" (Gopinath 1998).

Sita's statement that "there is no word in our language to describe what we are to each other" has been interpreted literally by critics like Roger Ebert to conclude that "lesbianism is so outside the experience of these Hindus that their language even lacks a word for it" (Ebert 1997). But, as Mona Bachmann points out, the "storm of commentary and counter commentary" about *Fire* proves Sita's statement wrong, because "while there maybe no adequate single word, there is certainly no shortage of words deployed to explain 'what we are' to interpret and reinterpret the fiery images on contemporary India's cultural screen" (Bachmann 2002, 43).

India's first public debate on homosexuality

Fire marks a significant moment in the history of sexual politics because it triggered the first public debate on homosexuality in independent India.[54] Reflecting upon the invisibility of lesbian women in literary and cinematic works, literary critic Terry Castle has written: "The lesbian is never with us, it seems, but always somewhere else: in the shadows, in the margins, hidden from history, out of sight, out of mind, a wanderer in the dusk, a lost soul, a tragic mistake, a pale denizen of the night" (Castle 1995, 2). It is in the

---

54. I use the term "independent India" advisedly because there have been at least two previous public debates on works related to homosexuality. In the 1920s, a public debate was triggered by a collection of Hindi short stories titled *Chocolate* (1927) by Pandey Bechan Sharma, a.k.a. Ugra. The public debate saw the participation of major public figures including the writer Premchand and Mahatma Gandhi (Vanita and Kidwai 2006, 280–87). In 1944, Chugtai's short story "Lihaf" was called obscene. The litigation caused a public furor, and Chugtai was asked to apologize. She refused, won the case, and "Lihaf" became a feminist cult classic. *Fire* is not an adaptation of "Lihaf" (Ghosh 2000).

world of vapors that the apparitional lesbian resides. In my review of *Fire* in 1999, I had written that female bonding, whether homosocial or homosexual, had been largely absent from Indian films. When it appeared fleetingly, it was only to disappear as quickly. If the "apparitional lesbian" of Indian films resided in the world of vapors, *Fire* was the first film to provide a body to the shadow-like subliminal lesbian. In that first review of the film, I had concluded: "For those in the audience waiting to see women in love, they need no longer read against the grain" (Ghosh 1999c). The theatrical release of *Fire* gave visibility to the representational lesbian, and the subsequent controversy gave visibility to the "real" lesbians. As a letter to *Manushi: A Journal about Women and Society* stated: "*Fire*'s most compelling point is the manner in which it has become a truly public text, the subject of controversy in the media and among viewers … The fact that it has elicited such strong reactions from critics and spectator is perhaps its most notable redeeming quality … For those of us who are lesbians, the film is a milestone because it has pushed the politics of same-sex love into the limelight with an unprecedented amount of publicity and hype" (Banerji 1999).

As the Hindu Right's violent offensive against *Fire* met with counter-protests from feminists, artists, filmmakers, human rights activists, and other members of civil society, a volatile public debate on queer sexuality was precipitated and circulated extensively through the media. Notably, this debate saw the emergence of a new constellation of interlocutors, the self-identified queer. This constituency brought to the public domain their demands for sexual rights. No longer were the counter-protests only about the freedom of speech and expression.

At the demonstration in front of the Regal Cinema on December 6, 1998, diverse groups of protestors came with their own list of priorities. The CALERI Citizens Report (1999) stated that "even as progressive, ant-communalist, ant-censorship coalitions formed to defend the film, the issue of sexuality was being lost under the so-called 'larger issues' of 'communalism' and 'censorship'" (4–6). Among those defending the right to free speech, many were wary of the final frontier—homosexuality. For instance, leftist theater activist Sudhanwa Deshpande's account of the Regal Cinema protest hints at this discomfort. He writes: "It is of course imperative for all secular people to protest such attacks. Secular and feminist organizations in the country including the Left did so unhesitatingly. And many of them did so for the principle and not necessarily because they particularly agreed with what the film was saying. As a matter of fact, some including myself and my colleagues in the Jana Natya Manch [a Delhi-based street-theater group] had not even seen the film when we defended its right to be shown" (Deshpande 2001).

As a participant at that event, I had written that the display of collective solidarity at the Regal Cinema counter-protest was not without discomfort around the visible and vocal presence of self-identified lesbians. Many of us recall that during and after the demonstration, several "progressives" openly disapproved of the fact that lesbians held placards that publicly announced their sexual orientation. Such a declaration was described through their use of words such as "excessive," "extreme," "sensational," and "irresponsible" (Ghosh 1999a). The implicit suggestion that lesbian women should have remained in the closet, even when the event being staged concerned their life and sexuality, bore ample evidence to how deeply entrenched heterosexism was, even among those who were publicly defending a film about lesbians.[55] Geeta Patel recalled that a banner that read, "We are Indians. Lesbianism is our Heritage" was described by a newspaper as having "screamed" the slogan. She wrote: "The verb *screamed* indicates how those who break the social contract of silence are heard" (Patel 2000, 230).

Different groups came to that demonstration with their own priorities. The lesbian groups demanded recognition for sexual rights while others foregrounded the right to free

---

55. S.L. wrote: "Some of us were taking great personal risks in holding up posters in the middle of a sea of candles, in the face of flashing cameras. Interestingly, some of the individuals and groups who had joined in to protest the attack on 'freedom of speech and expression' and 'democratic rights' were upset and vitriolic about the same freedoms being extended to a minority and in a peaceful and democratic protest. We were severely criticized before and after: why did we have to be visible?" (1999).

speech and expression. Both groups came with their own histories of silences and reservations about the other. Nonetheless, the counter-protest turned out to be a huge success and was reported extensively by the media. The coalition of multiple interlocutors served an affirmative purpose as each group gave tacit legitimacy to the other by virtue of sharing the same protest space.

If the newly emergent lesbian groups thought that they would find a natural ally in women's groups, they were mistaken. While some were quick to extend support, the left-wing women's groups were not easy to convince. As International Women's Day (March 8) approached, the issue of lesbian banners and slogans resurfaced again as a "problem" (Menon 2007, xiii–ix). The organizers of the annual event, dominated by left-wing women's groups, argued that "lesbian placards" would "cause confusion" and "divert attention" from the issues that were to be highlighted, in this case, the demolition of slums and dislocation of workers. The marginalization of sexual minorities continues to this day and is usually justified with the argument that there are many more pressing issues that need urgent attention. During the debate about lesbians' participation in the International Women's Day events, a senior member of a left-affiliated women's group informed me that while their organization would not advocate the rights of sexual minorities, it would certainly support lesbian women were they to become targets of violence. Besides suggesting a rather painful route to recognition, this stance demonstrated once again how lesbian women (like sex workers) could hope to get sympathy only if they were not active agents, but suffering victims. Nivedita Menon observes that "arguments about elitism and priority have historically been made by Left movements to counter feminism, and it is ironic that a new universal of Woman/Class was now being constituted by women's organizations of the Left against the destabilizing implications of homosexuality" (Menon 2007, 24).

In June 2001, *Himal* magazine carried a review of Rustom Bharucha's book *The Politics of Cultural Practice*. The reviewer, Sudhanva Deshpande, took issue with Bharucha's contention that secular constructions of political identity were implicitly heterosexist and that ideologies like Marxism were inflected by "patriarchal constructions of gender." Bharucha was predictably taken to task by Deshpande, who reasoned as follows:

> I would argue that once all differences and
> discriminations in society are assigned the same
> status and value, once the notion of a hierarchy
> of oppression is discarded, one loses all sense of
> proportion. After all, isn't it worth asking why
> groups (and intellectuals) which [*sic*] cry themselves
> hoarse about sexual politics never seem to be unduly
> perturbed when tribal activists are raped in Tripura?

> And if we are talking about the "costs and risks"
> which lesbians bear and their complex strategies of
> survival, why don't we also ... talk about the costs
> and risks, both sexual and social that *dalit* women
> agricultural workers bear and their complex strategies
> of survival? (Deshpande 2001)[56]

Deshpande's reference to the "costs and risks" taken by lesbian women was a response to Mary John and Tejaswini Niranjana's observation that heterosexual feminist and other democratic organizations in India show "few signs of being aware of the costs and risks lesbians bear on a daily basis in their private and professional lives" (1999). The homophobic myopia of the commentary not only confirms Rustom Bharucha's contention above, but also illustrates how lesbians and bisexual women have been "invisibilized" in the women's movement. The "natural" assumption seems to be that all women in the women's movement—that is, those who fight for the rights of Tribal women in Tripura or *dalit* agricultural workers—are, and always have been, heterosexual.

---

56. *Dalit* is a term of self-identification from people who have been traditionally regarded as "untouchables." It literally means "crushed under" or "trampled upon." *Dalit* people prefer this term to the euphemistic *harijan* (God's people) that Gandhi coined. Although the caste system was abolished by the Indian Constitution, prejudice and discrimination against *dalits* remains a harsh reality.

Where do lesbians come from?

Just as Deepa Mehta's *Fire* was embattled in a debate over nationality, so was queer sexuality in India. Was homosexuality Indian? Or was it an import? I must clarify at the very outset that indigenist claims hold no attraction for me. Had there been no historical evidence of homosexuality in India, I would unhesitatingly recommend its import like any other desirable commodity. However, there happens to be evidence to the contrary. Ruth Vanita and Saleem Kidwai's groundbreaking anthology *Same-Sex Love in India: Readings from Literature and History* (2001) conclusively shows that the legacy of same-sex love has been vibrant, diverse, and persistent in South Asian cultures. So while the matter is settled either way, the debate is worth revisiting because the discursive terrain over which this contestation plays out provides invaluable insights into the sexual politics of culture.

As we have seen, sexual speech was attacked by the Hindu Right as not only "vulgar and obscene" but as against "Indian culture." The controversy over *Fire* made this argument more acute. On November 22, 1998, the *Times of India* carried a full-page debate on homosexuality in which BJP ideologue K.R. Malkani wrote:

> Obviously, all this is part of the current rage for "modernization," globalization," "emancipation …
> Any rational being will concede that homosexuality is unnatural … However, there was always a strong

aversion to these perversions. When an Indian king
was defeated by Mahmud Ghazni, he was invited
to embrace Islam or face death. He said he could
become a Muslim to save his life but only if he was
not made to eat beef or sleep with a boy. When that
did not work out, he chose to immolate himself ...
[T]he presiding deities of globalization are already
thinking in terms of work for twenty percent and dole
for eighty percent; more profits, fewer jobs. In this
situation the unemployed majority will have nothing
else to do but entertain themselves with sex—any sex
... It is this death wish that has gripped millions in
the United States—and that threatens to engulf all
societies that go American. (Malkhani 1998)

In Malkani's paranoid formulation, heterosexuality "becomes a constant and natural presence that historically always requires protection from external threat, whether from
Muslims or globalization" (Desai 2002). Invoking the specter of "non-marriages, teenage mothers and single parent
families," Malkani prophesied that the "calamitous" outcome would include "neglected and traumatized children,"
who would end up as "morons, lunatics, criminals, or all
three combined." A group of academics from two of Delhi's
most prestigious universities promptly responded to Malkani and challenged his many contentions. In a letter to the
editor of the *Times of India* (December 6, 1998), they stated
that if homosexuality was "unnatural" then so were routine

activities like wearing clothes and cooking food—were these activities to be abandoned as well? They pointed out that given the evidence in folk and classical cultures including texts like *Manusmriti* and *Kamasutra*, it was futile to claim that homosexuality was "western." They critiqued Malkani's idea of a "god-given," immutable notion of the family by observing that sociological and historical studies indicate that family structures, like all human institutions, are subject to change. The letter concluded by stating: "It is time we came to terms with the diversities and complexities of co-existing sexual experiences—gay and lesbian existences, bisexuality, heterosexuality and celibacy."

A homophobic worldview was not restricted to the adherents of the Hindu Right alone. A senior columnist in the *Observer* warned that "people everywhere were deeply disturbed" about the relentless onslaught of "sex, smut, nudity, violence, filth and foulness" that was being beamed into people's homes through satellite TV, and against which the Shiv Sena attack on *Fire* could easily be read as an instance of legitimate anger. Warning Indians against the "Americanizing of Indian society and polity," the writer detailed a shopping list of deviants, including "a new generation of champions of the rights of bisexuals, homosexuals, lesbians, transvestites, prostitutes, pederasts, pornographers, drug-addicts, drug-peddlers, pop art, pop music, pop science, pop psychology, pop anthropology, and what not" (Uniyal 1998).

The anxiety about the "invasion of western moral values"

was replayed repeatedly through articles and letters to the editor.[57] The renowned Hindi writer Nirmal Verma declared that Deepa Mehta did not know anything about "lesbianism in Indian culture" and maintained that he had never come across any "lesbian or homosexual tradition in Indian culture" (in Subramanyam 1998). Fortuitously, Nishit Saran's auto-ethnographic documentary *Summer in My Veins* (1998) made its timely debut around the same time. Using an informal, home-video style, the film records Saran's coming out to his mother. It was a reply, as it were, to the Hindu Right's insistence that homosexuals did not exist in India. The queers were finally here to stay. As a well-known columnist wrote: "When you are heir to the breathtakingly permissive *Kamasutra*, why confine yourself to the missionary position on sexuality? … Homosexuality didn't need a visa to enter India, it was already here."[58]

The burgeoning evidence about the existence of homo-

---

57. In a letter to the editor of the *Pioneer* on December 14, 1998, Meera Prasad wrote: "In a society already tormented by the invasion of western moral values, where Indian parents are distraught by the practice of liberal sex among teenagers, one wonders how parents would extinguish the fire that would engulf their homes every day by this new 'liberal' trend!" In a letter to the *Times of India* on December 11, 1998, Pradep Kher wrote: "The obnoxious concept of a lesbian relationship in an Indian household as explicitly presented in the film is completely alien to our culture and traditions."

58. Bachi Kakaria, quoted in *CALERI report*, 1999, 16.

sexuality in South Asian cultures compelled the Hindu Right to add another position to their earlier stance. Reacting to the slogan "Lesbianism is part of our Heritage," Swapan Dasgupta, a journalist with a strong allegiance to the Hindu Right, stated: "Thievery, deceit, murder and other IPC [Indian Penal Code] defined offences have a long history. That doesn't elevate them to the level of heritage … Homosexuality may have found mention in some ancient manual and even depicted [*sic*] in a temple carving or two, but as in the pre-promiscuous West, it was a preference that was greeted with tolerant disapproval. It was always an alternative to marriage and family but never a socially acceptable option" (Dasgupta 1998). Dasgupta forgets to mention that many practices that we condemn today as discriminatory, violent, and misogynist were considered socially acceptable at one time.

Madhu Kishwar, a women's activist and editor of the journal *Manushi*, declared, in her scathing attack on *Fire*, that unlike the West, Indian society had "no comparable history of persecuting homosexuals," and that "India, despite more than two centuries of western influence and indoctrination, has still not become homophobic." She said: "I personally know any number of gay men and women, many of them in high profile professions. Not one has been fired from his or her job or made the butt of public ridicule." She goes on to state that Indian families tend to ignore relationships similar to Radha and Sita's, "provided people don't go around flaunting their sexual engagement with each other" (Kishwar 1998). In Kishwar's idyllic vision of Hindu India, homosexuality is accepted when it is invisible and lesbians are firmly stowed in the closet!

As the *Fire* controversy raged, a joke did the rounds in Delhi's feminist circles. It was being said that *Fire* had outed all lesbians by making it impossible for the homoerotic to pass as the homosocial. There was both anxiety and affection in the circulation of this joke. Kishwar warned that "there is a danger that many of those exposed to this controversy will learn to view all such signs of affection through the prism of homosexuality. As a consequence many women may feel inhibited in expressing physical fondness for other women for fear of being branded as lesbians." Homophobic anxieties such as these were commonly expressed but were countered by both queer and non-queer feminists. In a seminar where I presented a paper on queer literary texts, a leading feminist scholar remarked that *Fire* had "vulgarized" interpretations of physicality between women by leading people to conclude that such contacts were necessarily sexual. Another feminist was quick to point out that perhaps the "vulgarity" lay in concluding that all such contact was necessarily non-sexual.

Fire *amidst culture wars*

The re-release of *Fire* allowed the film to be discussed and the text revisited outside the context of free speech and cultural emergency. The *Economic and Political Weekly* pub-

FIGURE 22. Jatin is open about his extramarital affair with Julie. DVD still.

lished a series of articles that debated the sexual and cultural politics of *Fire*. "Does our whole hearted opposition to the Shiv Sena protests require that we celebrate the film?" asked Mary John and Tejaswini Niranjana in an essay that critiqued the film for being a simplistic, radical-feminist project that represented "patriarchy as founded on the denial of female sexuality." In their words, "[The] reduction of woman to her body is accompanied by the equation of patriarchy with Indian culture and tradition, epitomized by the imprisonment of Radha and Sita (later changed to Nita) within the confines of the Hindu joint family." According to John and Niranjana, *Fire* seemed to suggest "that the successful assertion of sexual choice is not only a necessary but also a sufficient condition—indeed the sole criterion—

for the emancipation of women" (1999, 581).

In a thoughtful response, Ratna Kapur argued that while their position possibly reflected one way of interpreting the film, it was by no means the only one. Kapur does not see the film as making any claims to simple universal truths or notions about the cause of women's oppression. On the contrary, she usefully points out that the film ends ambiguously as the women learn the "pleasures and persecutions that result in being involved in a lesbian relationship with one's sister-in-law in a joint Hindu family." Therefore, it would be reductive to read the film as unproblematically valorizing sexual choice (more specifically, lesbian choice) and the subsequent "unfettered liberation of all women."[59] Kapur argued that *Fire* represents how culture is "confused, contradictory and uneven":

> It is within the cultural space of the Hindu joint
> family that that the relationship between the women
> develops, where "Hindu" tales and stories provide
> Mundu with fodder for his fantasies, in particular
> about winning Radha's heart. Hindi popular culture
> provides the space for the [women] to dance away in
> drag before their mute mother-in-law, who is clearly
> amused by their performance. It is within this very

59. Kapur refuses to use the term "patriarchy," arguing that it is a "historical, universal term that has little explanatory value." I avoid the term for the same reason.

cultural space that Jatin sells his porn and also has
an extramarital relationship. Indeed the only person
in the script who appears to believe that there is one
big happy joint Hindu family, that there exists a static
notion of culture, is Ashok. Sitting with his utterly
deviant family in Lodhi Gardens he states: "I am
lucky to have such a good family." (Kapur 1999)

The film's portrayal of Hinduism has been a point of dis-
putation. Madhu Kishwar attacked *Fire* as a "mean spirited
caricature of middle class families among urban Hindus"
and "an exercise in self-flagellation by a self-hating Hindu
and a self-despising Indian" (Kishwar 1999).[60] Since Kishwar has a strong affinity to Hindu nationalism, her positions
are often indistinguishable from that of the Hindu Right.
But a similar criticism, albeit from a different vantage point,
has also come from those who have been strongly supportive
of the film. Ruth Vanita's only major criticism of the film,
for instance, is that it "launches an unnecessary and ill-con-
ceived critique of Hinduism" (Vanita and Kidwai 2000, 244).
I am not sure that the film seeks to target "Hinduism" as
much as it seeks to critique upper-caste Hindu beliefs and

60. Kishwar is an unstable ally of gay/lesbian issues. During TV
debates after the Delhi High Court decriminalized homosexuality,
Kishwar staunchly defended the judgement even though her
arguments tended to be unconventional. Every time homosexuality
was described as "unnatural," she would demand that a certificate
from "Nature" be produced testifying to the same.

practices like Karva Chauth, of which feminists have had a longstanding critique.[61] While I have no doubts that Mehta's ironic take on Hindu practices may have hurt some people (as there is no speech that does not offend someone), it cannot be denied that the irreverence delighted many of us who were exhausted by the Hindu Right's domination of political and cultural spaces. As a film that was planned, shot, and released during a decade that saw the political rise of the Hindu Right, *Fire* became an important intervention in the debate on secularism, democratic dissent, and the rights of minorities.

In view of the Hindu Right's political deployment of the *Ramayana*, Mehta's use of the same serves a cinematic and political purpose. In the late 1980s and '90s, the Hindu Right launched a nationwide campaign to liberate the birthplace of mythical deity Ram. Drawing its visual metaphors from the *Ramayana*, Hindu Right chose as its primary iconography the image of a muscular and fully armed Ram who is ready to wage war. Any other iconography that challenged this one interpretation came under attack. In 1993, for example, Hindu Right groups launched a vicious campaign against

---

61. Asked why *Fire* had been set in a Hindu household, Deepa Mehta said: "A majority of films made in India are set in Hindu households. Besides, I am a Hindu and the particular milieu of *Fire* is a milieu with which I am familiar and feel comfortable portraying. It is like asking Ismat Chughtai (posthumously) to change the milieu of *Lihaf* from a Muslim household into a Hindu one" (Azmi 1998).

SAHMAT (the Safar Hashmi Memorial Trust, a secular cultural organization), which had mounted an exhibition on the many folk and classical versions of the *Ramayana* in order to promote a more syncretic idea of India's diverse cultural traditions.[62] One particular folk version that depicted Ram and Sita as siblings came under furious attack. The exhibition was vandalized on the pretext that Hindu sentiments had been hurt by this "vulgar" suggestion. The police refused to apprehend the vandals; instead, they confiscated the offending panel and slapped a number of criminal charges on SAHMAT.

The *agni pariksha* reference that Mehta uses as a recurrent motif in the film centers around Ram's insistence that Sita prove her purity by immersing herself in fire. In the popular imagination, Sita is an embodiment of duty, self-sacrifice, and idealized femininity. Therefore, it is ironic (and fitting) that in the *Ramayana* performance at Swamiji's ashram, the role of Sita should be played by a transgender actor. As the local actors play out their version, Swamiji watches attentively while Ashok divides his attention between watching the play and swatting insects that venture too close to his

62. The exhibition was hosted by SAHMAT, an organization founded in memory of Safdar Hashmi, a left-wing cultural activist who was killed by assassins allegedly hired by a certain Congress leader who has been accused of instigating mob attacks on the Sikhs in the aftermath of Indira Gandhi's assassination by a Sikh bodyguard.

guru. In the play, the transgender Sita walks through card-board flames only to be told by Ram that, even though she was proven pure, she must nevertheless be exiled. Having performed this sequence many times, the onstage Sita does not seem distressed, but Swamiji is moved to tears by what most of us would imagine to be Sita's tragic plight—until he sighs, "Poor Ram."

It is also useful to remember that *Fire* does not only critique Hindu myths and traditions but reclaims them through feminist subversion. The Karva Chauth sequence is perhaps the best example. Similarly, the trial by fire is a reworking of the popular mythical version. In a metaphoric reversal, it is not Sita who undergoes the test of purity but Radha who, like her mythical namesake, surmounts innumerable obstacles to be united with her lover. For once, it is not Sita who has to undergo trial by fire but for whom it is undertaken.

The symbolism in *Fire* is drawn not only from Hindu myths and legends, but also from Sufism. Unlike orthodox Islam, Sufism (Islamic mysticism) emphasizes personal devotion against a rigid fidelity to dogma.[63] Since love is central to Sufi spiritualism, music, and poetry, the relationship between divine and human is often articulated through homoerotic metaphors. The film ends with the women re-

---

63. For an excellent discussion on Sufism, see "Introduction: Medieval Materials in the Perso-Urdu Tradition" in Vanita and Kidwai, *Same-Sex Love in India*.

FIGURE 23. Radha and Sita pray for a life together at the Nizamuddin shrine. DVD still.

united at the shrine of Hazrat Nizamuddin Auliya, where, earlier in the film, they had prayed for a life together. Sufi shrines have historically provided refuge and nurturance to same-sex couples, but the Nizamuddin shrine has a special significance because of its association with Amir Khusrow, the mystic poet-musician par excellence, and his deep bond with his spiritual mentor, Nizamuddin.[64]

Madhu Kishwar took exception to the choice of spaces in

---

64. Amir Khusrow (1253–1325) produced a voluminous body of work in both Persian and Hindvi. His Hindvi poetry was developed through his deep and intense association with Nizamuddin. Khusrow died a few months after the death of his beloved Nizamuddin, and their tombs lie side-by-side at the Delhi shrine.

the film.""All the scenes associated with Hindu spaces and symbols are sites of oppression," wrote Kishwar, while the family's "one and only happy outing," is at a garden built around a Muslim monument." Sita and Radha's "moment of freedom and liberation" and "final union," moreover, takes place at the Nizamuddin shrine (1998). Kishwar's reference to the Lodhi Gardens is both misleading and curious as the gardens function primarily as a public park surrounding a medieval monument built by a Muslim ruler. The sprawling lawns are regularly frequented by people of different class, caste, religious, and ethnic backgrounds and cannot by any stretch of the imagination be described as a "Muslim space." The Nizamuddin *dargah* could be described as one, but again, Sufi shrines are known for their appeal to diverse communities of people, which explains Radha and Sita's original visit to the shrine.

With a different political perspective, Urdu scholar C.M. Naim makes an observation similar to Kishwar's. He objects to the *dargah* as a site of reunion because "it sets up a totally false and possibly dangerous dichotomy between Hinduism and Sufism/Islam. The former becomes all cold, unfeeling and hypocritical; the latter all warm and caring." He says the film would have benefited had Mehta "looked into some of the *bhakti* and other devotional traditions available within the umbrella of Hinduism" (1999). Kishwar feels that the women should have checked into a hotel or gone to a Gurdwara (a Sikh house of worship) where they would have received both shelter and free food. Both Kishwar and Naim, albeit for different reasons, seem to be asking Mehta to not stray from her own territory, thereby reinforcing the unhelpful binary they set out to condemn. In a film where many borders are crossed and many conventions transgressed, it is entirely fitting that Mehta's female protagonists should stake claim to a tradition they did not inherit through the accident of birth.[65] While Naim is derisive about such syncretism, I would argue that by choosing a Sufi *dargah*, Mehta has refused to define Indian culture solely as Hindu culture. This is particularly important because queer groups have frequently (often, inadvertently) invoked a glorious Hindu past to authenticate their existence to the exclusion of other cultures. The repeated references to texts like the *Kamasutra*, *Manusmriti*, and the Khajuraho erotic temple sculptures have reinforced the history of homosexuality in India as predominantly a Hindu one. For example, Giti Thadani's work on excavating a lesbian past in Indian history relies heavily on a Hindu nationalist framework (Thadani, 1999).

---

65. In the same essay, Naim took issue with me for having described Khusrow and Nizamuddin's relationship as "homoerotic." It is true that there is no evidence to "prove" the veracity of such a claim. However, the stories about their intense attachment combined with the romantic tropes and metaphors used in Sufi poetry—including those attributed to Khusrow—allow for such a reading. This is not to suggest that my reading is the definitive one.

This bias was finally corrected when, in 2000, Vanita and Kidwai's groundbreaking anthology on same-sex love was published.

Geeta Patel's observation that *Fire* reads very differently in North America than in South Asia suggests the role that historical circumstances play in responding to a film—even though such responses are by no means universal or monolithic. She noted that, in the US and Canada, Mehta was repeatedly asked to account for her representation of men and masculinity. During the controversy on *Fire*, Patel initiated a discussion with her students at the American college where she teaches. One of the college's benefactors objected to the screening of *Fire* at the college and threatened to withdraw financial support. Patel's students—who were mostly white—seemed strangely reticent to debate the controversy. Patel discovered that the head of the Indian students' association, a non-resident Indian woman, disliked the representation of men in the film. "The voice of the designated 'other,'" Patel wrote, "has spoken her will through a speaking of her injury." Patel quotes Berlant, who has pointed out that "the other's injured self will win out because the discourse of personal injury seems impassable." Reflecting upon how the "bad representation" of men wounds women in the diaspora, she suggested that South Asian anxieties around the bodies of men in *Fire* played out in a context of racial and ethnic tensions having to do with "raced bodies" being returned to the circuit of "failure." What cannot be spoken, says Patel, is that "virile heteromasculinity is fully implicated in a right-wing production of proper masculine citizenship." Consequently, the debate on the representation of men and masculinities in *Fire* is resolved very differently within the different contexts of India and the diaspora.

John and Niranjana claim that *Fire*'s "subversive potential" is "nullified by its largely masculinist assumption that men should not neglect the sexual needs of their wives lest they turn lesbian" (1999). They observe that "the narrative is set in motion by the negative, even traumatic sexual experiences of the two sisters-in-law in their respective marital relationships: Radha who is infertile has to contend with a celibate husband who must also 'test' his celibacy in bed; [Sita's] boorish husband has rough sexual intercourse with her after marriage, but spends the rest of the time with his girlfriend." Author and socialite Shobha De thought the film was an "insult to lesbians" because it celebrated a "rejection vote." Blaming the film for showing lesbianism as a "decision based on default not choice," she wrote, "I hate to think that women only gravitate towards one another (physically and emotionally) because nobody else wants them. Because it's the second best option" (De, 1998). As Brinda Bose asked in her essay on *Fire*, "How powerful is a choice if it emerges out of expediency?" (Bose 2007, 439).

Refuting John and Niranjana's contention that the viewer is left with an "overall sense of sexual victimization,"

Ratna Kapur has argued that "the story of victimization is hardy unusual in Indian films" and points out the many moments of agency displayed by the women: "I do not agree that the film is making an unambiguous statement that the women fall into a lesbian relationship as a result of bad marriages ... Mundu was there for the taking—he was ready and willing, if only Radha had made the first overture" (Kapur 1999).

That neither husband should have any romantic or sexual interest in their wives might allow the narrative to fold back into a homophobic interpretative scheme by implying that the women became lesbians only when denied heterosexual love. But, as other commentators have pointed out, this is only one of the readings that the film makes available. Gayatri Gopinath argues that, given the middle-class urban context the film details, "it is precisely within the cracks and fissures of rigidly heteronormative arrangements that queer female desire can emerge." Like the women in Ismat Chugtai's "Lihaf," Radha and Sita are able to extricate themselves from the terms of patriarchal heteronormativity by creating their own circuits of pleasure, desire, and fantasy (Gopinath 2005, 153).

The relationship of the two women is developed painstakingly over several sequences testifying to a number of explorations that bring them together. When, in an interview with *Trikone* magazine, Mehta was asked whether her narrative implies that "lesbianism isn't anything that a good man can't cure," she replied: "I am talking about the nature of passion, and passion can erupt in the most unlikely places, unlikely circumstances, and between the most unlikely people. In this case, it did erupt in unlikely circumstances, in the middle of a joint family in New Delhi, between two sisters-in-law ... If they had been satisfied by their males, would it have happened? Perhaps not this way, it might have happened another way. For me these women were bound to fall in love at some point because their spirits were calling out to each other" (Kamani 1997).

The trouble in persisting with the "bad-husbands-cause-lesbianism" interpretation is that it casts Sita and Radha as victims to the total disregard of their will and agency in initiating and sustaining what turns into a passionate love affair. If anything, their love story demonstrates that, in any journey of empowerment, the destination is more important than the place of departure. To this end, Radha and Sita's story is no different from the many stories of empowerment that begin from a place of unhappiness or trauma.[66]

The most complex male figure in the film is Mundu, who does not lend himself to any easy readings. John and

66. There are innumerable films that have shown transgressive choices emerging from traumatic situations. For instance, *Ek Baar Phir* (*Once Again*, Vinod Pande, 1980) was the first Bombay film to support a women's decision to affirm an extra-marital relationship. The fact that the husband was boorish and self-centered did not lead audiences to protest that the wife had settled for a "default option."

Niranjana read Mundu's character as revealing the hidden class bias of the film, with the women's sexuality being valorized against the "vilified sexuality" of the servant. The class-caste prejudices of the film, in their opinion, are played out through a series of contrasts: the women are treated with "high seriousness" while the male servant provides "comic relief"; the "lighting and camera angles play up the women's beauty and satirize the servant as misshapen" (John and Niranjana, 1999). While this last observation may be an instance of gross over-reading, Mundu is a figure through whom Mehta's own class biases begin to be understood (Deshpande 2001). Unable to construe Mundu into the film's sexual politics, C. M. Naim sardonically asks: "Is he just another despicable male, or is he an exploited human being? Or is there a parallel suggestion between him and the two women …" (1999).

After Mundu is caught masturbating, there is a sequence in which Radha sits on the terrace and reflects about herself in the light of Mundu's sexual transgression. "Mundu did not think of anyone but himself," she says. "Is it wrong to be so selfish?" She wonders if she is, in fact, any different from him. Radha then tells Sita that "this awareness of needs and desires" is new for her. This sequence does not lend itself to any easy "unpacking," simply because the points of comparison are obscure. What do Radha and Mundu's sexual transgressions have in common? Both can be seen as violations of trust, both provoke outrage and risk social stigma.

FIGURE 24. The Karva Chauth story plays out in Mundu's imagination, as does his crush on Radha. (Courtesy: Nandita Das)

Yet the comparisons do not really hold, given their differing circumstances and social status in the household. Consequently, any interpretation of this sequence resists certainty.

Mehta herself describes Mundu as her *sutradhar* (the storyteller who holds the narrative strands together) and Greek chorus: "He is very aware, as servants are in India, especially when you're sharing a very small space. [He is] the only one who goes from bedroom to bedroom and who has access to everybody's private life. But because it's very inconvenient to pay attention to him, because we would never be able to use him we choose to keep a distance from his or her needs" (Kamani 1997).

Mundu resists easy categorization; he works like a slave, has no time for leisure, and the only treat he can afford is to hurriedly masturbate in front of Biji, the one family member who can't squeal on him. Mehta describes him as "bored out of his mind; he's not treated like a human being, he works like a dog, and he wants some recreation time … and he probably gets very little … And he's also got a major crush on Radha"[67] (ibid). Mundu has discerned that his only hope of surviving in an unequal system is to deploy a number of performative strategies that range from being helpless to downright devious. When Radha catches him masturbating in front of Biji, he quickly adopts a number of personas to overcome the crisis: Having failed to elicit Radha's sympathy through an account of his wretched existence, he does a quick turnaround and threatens to disclose her relationship with Sita. When Jatin almost hits him for disclosing his ownership of the porn videos, Mundu pacifies him with flattery. That evening, as the family sits down to watch the *Ramayana* (in what seems to be a group therapy situation),

---

67. Mundu's unrequited love for Radha could well be a point of identification for many queer and straight viewers who are familiar with situations of impossible longing and transgressive love. In many families, inter-caste and inter-class relationships would provoke as much opposition as queer love. India continues to witness inter-caste killings (euphemistically called honour killings) in which people who dare to marry outside their caste or community are killed, often by family members.

FIGURE 25. Of all the characters in the film, Mundu is the most difficult
to read. DVD still.

Mundu throws himself at Biji's feet in a display of histri-
onics. When Ashok banishes Mundu, he first maintains a
stoic silence, then shows anger, and finally, abject misery.
Unfortunately, the artful dodger's last gamble does not pay
off. As Ratna Kapur writes, Mundu is rejected "not when he
is chastised for masturbating in front of the television and
the old mother but when he reveals the 'hanky-panky' of the
sisters-in-law to Ashok. He is cast out for daring to reveal
the misdeeds of his 'madams' rather than perpetrating his
own sexual misdeeds" (1999).

Showing both vulnerability and agency, Mundu remains
one of the most complex characters in the story, one whose
persona is textured through contradictions and instabilities.
The discomfort that many viewers have felt with him could

have to do with the impossibility of being able to place him as either victim or villain. Ranjit Chowdhry's subtly nuanced performance compels the viewer to regard Mundu with uncertainty and ambivalence and through the lens of our own conflicted feelings regarding people of a different caste and class who share our homes but not our privileges.

CONCLUSION: WHY *FIRE* HAS CHANGED OUR WAYS OF LOOKING

Learning to look queerly

Fire opens with a gentle exhortation to "see what you can't see" and to "see without looking." The mustard field sequences are both a memory and a dreamscape that shapes Radha's selfhood, her relationship with Sita, and perhaps even her destiny. It is a reminder "of wide open spaces, of the sea beyond the limits of the land, of the need to see without looking" (Jain 2009, 58). In addition to the literal references to seeing, *Fire* can be read as a parable on looking and an allegory about spectatorship. Referring to the film's recurring mustard-field sequence, Gayatri Gopinath says it suggests an analogy "with the ways in which *Fire* interrogates the notion that the proper location of lesbianism is within a politics of visibility in the public sphere" (2005, 140).

Let's return to the picnic sequence where the irony of Sita massaging Radha's feet is evident to the audience but not to the husbands. While one husband encourages his wife to go right ahead with the massage, the other congratulates himself on having such a "good" family. The brothers could well be the spectators whose heteronormatively circumscribed imagination renders invisible all signs of queer desire, even when plainly visible. This inability to "see" while looking

FIGURE 26. Retrospectatorship allows us to read back and into.
Superstars Amitabh Bachchan and Rajesh Khanna in *Namak Haram*
(1973). DVD still. © R.S.J. Productions

may be why non-queer spectators often ask their queer
counterparts, "But aren't you reading 'too much' into the
text?"

With few exceptions, representations of female bonding,
unlike male bonding, were largely absent from popular Indian cinema until the turn of the twenty-first century. Female
bonding has almost always lacked the vitality of male bonding. Female homoeroticism appeared fleetingly in films such
as *Razia Sultan* (*Queen Razia*, Kamal Amrohi, 1983), *Mere
Mehboob* (*My Beloved*, Harnam Singh Rawail, 1963), *Humjoli*

(*Beloved Friend*, Ramanna, 1970), and Y*eh Aag Kab Bujhegi* (*When Will This Fire Be Doused?* Sunil Dutt, 1991), as well as more self-consciously in Shyam Benegal's *Mandi* (*Marketplace*, 1983), but rarely was it central to the male-dominated narratives of popular cinema. Barring films that privileged the heroine, as in the genre of courtesan films, women never enjoyed the narrative centrality that male protagonists did. It was only in the 1990s that this began to change.

Fire qualifies as a queer classic because it is the first Indian film to bring women in love out of the margins and into the mainstream and to provide a body to the shadow-like subliminal lesbian of film narratives in India. But more importantly, *Fire* inaugurates a new interpretive strategy by explicitly crossing the line between female homosociality and female homosexuality (Ghosh 2002). Routine homosocial activities such as cooking, hanging clothes to dry, or oiling each other's hair become invested with sexual and erotic energy. Such activities are no longer what they appear to be. Gayatri Gopinath has noted how the film produces a complicated relay between female homosociality and female homoerotic practices. She describes the sequence in which Sita massages Radha's feet at the family picnic as "transforming a daily female homosocial activity into an intensely homoerotic one" (1998, 635). Similarly, the scene in which Sita oils Radha's hair becomes erotically charged with in view of their sexual involvement.

The homosocial activities that Radha and Sita engage in

are commonly witnessed in life as in films. By framing these activities in social, romantic, erotic, and finally, explicitly sexual contexts, the film inscribes images of homosociality with an ambiguity that dislocates any deterministic reading of them as necessarily heterosexual. This interpretive strategy, privileged in queer subcultures, now enters the public domain, altering forever mainstream spectatorial practices. From now on, queers and non-queers alike are destined to read "too much" into the text.

This new interpretative strategy facilitates the reclamation of older texts through newer ways of reading where reading back is inevitably reading into (White 1999, 197).[68] This retro-spectatorship makes available a number of films where, heterosexual love interests notwithstanding, same-sex love and friendship are central to the plot. Films including *Dosti* (*Friendship*, Satyen Bose, 1964), *Anand* (*Joy*, Hrishikesh Mukherjee, 1971) *Namak Haram* (*The Traitor*, Hrishikesh Mukherjee, 1973) *Sholay* (*Embers*, Ramesh Sippy, 1975), *Anurodh* (*Request*, Shakti Samanta, 1977), *Yaraana* (*Friendship*, Rakesh Kumar, 1981), *Naam* (*Name*, Mahesh Bhatt, 1986), and *Main Khiladi Tu Anari* (*I Am the Expert and You're Amateur*, Sameer Malkan, 1994) can be—and have been—opened out for new readings (Waugh 2001, 280–97).

---

68. White recalls viewing practices attached to film retrospectives, "through which texts of the past, reordered and contextualized, are experienced in a different film-going culture" (1999, 197).

This process is generously aided by Bombay cinema's long-standing convention of staging love and friendship through similar and overlapping tropes of intimacy—gazing, touching, and embracing—as well as passionate declarations of love and commitment. Bombay cinema's expressions of intimacy have, in the words of Lauren Berlant, relied heavily on "the shifting registers of unspoken ambivalence" (2000, 7). My idea is not to suggest that retro-spectatorship be applied unproblematically to queer texts but used to demonstrate "what is precarious and lacking in heterosexual meaning" (Gandhi 2002, 95).[69]

Queerness in cinema after Fire

The coming out of cinematic queerness at the turn of the millennium witnessed two major currents. The first was the start of a new queer cinema that displaced conventional codes of masculinity and femininity. Inspired by independent film movements and emergent sexual politics, films such as *Shabnam Mausi* (*Shabnam Aunty*, Yogesh Bhardwaj, 2005) and *My Brother Nikhil* (Onir, 2005) are bold incursions into queer lives. The second, more predominant current signals the emergence of an ambivalent discourse that invokes queer desires through a simultaneous address to the

---

69. Taking this cue from the work of Christopher Lane, Leela Gandhi adopts this approach to read poet/novelist Vikram Seth's work queerly.

erotic and the phobic. It is possible that this ambivalence is contoured by the public dilemma around emergent sexualities and a struggle to come to terms with it.

The template for the coming out of cinematic queerness was provided not by Deepa Mehta's *Fire* but Gurinder Chadha's *Bend It Like Beckham* (2002). Released in Hindi and English, the film shows two football buddies, Jaswinder (Parminder Nagra) and Juliette/a.k.a. Jules (Keira Knightly), who are mistaken for lesbian lovers. The comedy of errors begins when the homophobic mother of the English girl begins misreading their buddy bonding and passionate fights—ironically, over a male football coach. Parminder's family (Indians settled in Britain) mistake Jules for a boy and raise hell. The family is pacified when the "boy" in question turns out to be a girl. On the other hand, Juliette's mother is hysterical because she is convinced that her daughter is a lesbian, Parminder's family is blissfully oblivious to the possibility of homosexuality.[70] When Juliette's angry mother hurls the word "lesbian" accusingly at Parminder during a family wedding, a bewildered elderly aunt says, "Lesbian? But she's born in March. I thought she's Piscean!" Another high-handedly adds, "She's not Lebanese, she's Punjabi."

The mistaken sexual identities of the two women and the responses of their respective families account for much

---

70. The "knowing" English family and the "unaware" Indian family reinforce the idea that homosexuality is alien to Indian cultures.

FIGURE 27. The erotic and the phobic in *Kal Ho Na Ho* (2003). The homophobic housekeeper spots the "queers" who happen to be actors Shah Rukh Khan and Saif Ali Khan. DVD still. © Dharma Productions

of the humor in the film, which nevertheless is careful not to let the lines between homosociality and homoeroticism blur. It is said that Chadha originally conceived the film as a lesbian love story but had to change the script to make it more marketable for the producers. Consequently, sexual ambiguity is displaced in favor of unambiguous straightness on the part of the two female protagonists. Contrary to all appearances, the film seems to suggest, these smart, masculine women playing a butch game are actually femmes. An irate Juliette defensively tells her mother, "Just because I wear trackkies and play sports does not make me a lesbian."

This trope of false appearances and mistaken identities becomes popular cinema's preferred way to sight the queer and finds its most successful expression in Nikhil Advani's Bollywood blockbuster *Kal Ho Naa Ho* (*If Tomorrow Never Comes*, 2003). A love triangle involving two men and one

FIGURE 28. The first kiss (performed by actors John Abraham and Abhishekh Bachchan) between male protagonists in any Bombay film. Notwithstanding criticism, *Dostana* (2008) has become a queer cult classic. DVD still. © Dharma Productions

woman, the film plays self-consciously on the slippage between friendship and eroticism but retains an ambivalent attitude toward homosexuality by incorporating a disapproving homophobe in the figure of a paranoid housekeeper who becomes paralyzed with terror every time she "misreads" the physical intimacies of the two men. Similarly, a homophobic sexologist in *Masti* (*Pranks*, Indra Kumar, 2004) is thrown into panic by a series of (accidental and staged) queer misreadings. The same idea is played out in *Housefull* (Sajid Khan, 2010). Since these readings hinge on the idea of false appearances and mistaken identities, the motivation for laughter remains resolutely ambiguous. Are we laughing at homophobia or at homosexuality? While the text allows viewers to occupy a variety of reading positions, it is worth noting that, in these films, it is the homophobe who becomes the sighter of queers and the interpreter of queer readings.

Dostana (*Friendship*, Tarun Mansukhani, 2008) marks a significant shift by building the gag of misreading into an integral plot element while de-centering the key role played by the homophobe. It is no longer the on-screen homophobe who misreads (or reads) but the on-screen queers. The earlier preoccupation with simultaneously invoking the phobic and the erotic is displaced when the homophobic mother, who fails to exorcise the ghost of gayness from her son, finally accepts his imagined (or real) sexuality. The rapturous climax features the first kiss between male protagonists in any Bombay film. At the end of the film, it is likely that the spectators (like the on-screen protagonists) will be "haunted" by the specter of the kiss and a sneaking suspicion that things may well be what we fear they are!

Endnote

The strategies of staging cinematic queerness in contemporary Bollywood's lavish blockbusters are poised precisely on the brink of knowing the slippage that *Fire* so forcefully articulates. At the same time, the deployment of the ambivalent tropes of the phobic and the erotic through false appearances and mistaken identities reveals a hesitancy in adopting *Fire*'s direct strategy of representing the queer. It bears noting that films like *My Brother Nikhil* and *Shabnam Mausi*, which are stylistically closer to the realism of *Fire*

FIGURE 29. The DVD cover of *Girlfriend* (2004). © S. P. Creations

than the non-realism of Bollywood, maintain a discreet reticence about rendering visible the sex lives of their queer protagonists. The gay love story of *My Brother Nikhil* is narrated through the tropes of homosociality while the eponymous Shabnam Mausi's relationship with a male lover ends early in the film.

The only other popular film to have unambiguously visibilized lesbian love-making has been the controversial *Girlfriend* (Karan Razdan, 2004). If the queer-identified spectator first emerged publicly during the *Fire* controversy, it was the debate around *Girlfriend* that first ruptured essentialist constructions of queer-identified spectatorship, thereby signaling the complex negotiation that attends the reading of any cinematic representation. The release of *Girlfriend* met with strong but peaceful protests by queer activists who were justifiably enraged by the film's sexual politics and its mobilizing of prejudicial myths about lesbian women. Just as the film was being attacked for articulating a right-wing position on lesbian sexuality, the Hindu Right attacked the film for promoting homosexuality. How could the same film outrage two such opposing constituencies? I have suggested elsewhere that an answer may lie in the narrative being positioned on the precarious faultline of the phobic and the erotic (Ghosh 2007, 417–36). The homophobic storyline notwithstanding, the film clearly renders visible the romantic and sexual possibilities of women loving women, including two extended lesbian love-making sequences. The first sequence appears in flashback as the reluctant lesbian (now reformed hetero) confesses to an evening of intoxicated (and intoxicating) lesbian sex. The second, equally explicit love-making sequence turns out to be a nightmare from which the hero wakes up and resolves to "save" the girlfriend by marrying her. Both sequences are visualized through the imaginings of not the dreaded lesbian but of the seemingly straight, even homophobic, characters. Once again, it is the homophobe who provides access to the erotic world of queer love.

In contrast, *Men Not Allowed* (Shrey Srivastava, 2006), a

FIGURE 30. The lesbian relationship in *Men Not Allowed* (2006) plays out on the borderline of friendship and erotica. DVD still. © Shri Vardan Pictures

lesbian love story with a happy and affirmative ending, shows no explicit love-making between the two women. This fact would have been unremarkable had the film not been punctuated by sex scenes featuring heterosexual couples, including the two female protagonists and their male lovers. While the straight-sex sequences are resonant of soft-porn film conventions, lesbian love is represented through the classic tropes of the romantic melodrama. The conclusion of *Girlfriend*, unlike that of *Men Not Allowed*, reaffirms heterosexuality and punishes the lesbian woman with death. Yet it is able to create narrative space for visibilizing lesbian sexual pleasure. *Men Not Allowed*, its privileging of lesbian love notwithstanding, invisibilizes lesbian sex. (*Fire*'s framing of sexual explicitness using the parenthesis of bad marriages may well have been an extension of the same logic.)

The business of looking has never been easy, but looking at queer cinema may be particularly fraught as the narrative logic of visibilizing the queer may, on occasion, run counter to the logic of sexual politics on the ground (Ghosh 2010). Very different rules and conventions govern the worlds of representation. As is evident from the discussion above, *Fire* has had no significant successor. After *Fire*, no other film released in India, has rendered visible queer love through simultaneously deploying the sexual explicitness of realist narratives and the tropes of romantic melodrama popularized by Bombay cinema. Nor has any other film so resolutely refused to consent to heteronormative domesticity and the prevailing social contract of heterosexuality. These attributes make *Fire* an unavoidable ghostly intertext. Even when a film with a queer theme tries to not be *Fire*, it invokes its memory through its absence. Like the apparitional lesbian, the presence and absence of *Fire* will continue to haunt and inhabit spaces of queer and non-queer love.

REFERENCES

Azmi, Shabana. 1998. Freedom under fire: Smokescreen for hidden
   agenda. *Times of India*, December 17.

Bachmann, Mona. 2002. After the fire. In *Queering India: Same-sex love
   and eroticism in Indian culture and society*, ed. Ruth Vanita. 234–43. New
   York: Routledge.

Banerji, Rima. 1999. Still on fire. *Manushi* 113 (July–August): 18–19.

Banning, Kass. 1999. Playing in the light: Canadianizing race and nation.
   In *Gendering the nation: Canadian women's cinema*, eds. Kay Armatage, et
   al. 291–310. Toronto: University of Toronto Press.

Bose, Brinda. 2007. The desiring subject: Female pleasures and feminist
   resistance in Deepa Mehta's *Fire*. In *The phobic and the erotic: The politics
   of sexualities in contemporary India*, eds. Brinda Bose and Subhabrata
   Bhattacharyya. 437–50. Calcutta: Seagull Books.

Campaign for Lesbian Rights (CALERI). 1999. *Lesbian emergence: A
   citizen's report*. New Delhi: [privately published].

Castle, Terry. 1995. *The apparitional lesbian: female homosexuality and
   modern culture*. New York: Columbia University Press.

Chakrabarty, Dipesh. 2000. *Provincializing Europe: Postcolonial thought and
   historical difference*. Princeton, NJ: Princeton University Press.

Comer, Brooke. 1997. *Fire* sets traditional Indian family values
   ablaze: shooting *Fire*, a film about a New Delhi family. *American
   Cinematographer*. (January): 99–100.

Cuthbert, Pamela. 1996. Deepa Mehta's trial by fire. *Take One*

(December–February): 29–31. Dasgupta, Swapan. 1998. [untitled]. *India Today* (December 21).

De, Shobha. 1999. An insult to lesbians. *The Week* (January 3).

Desai, Jigna. 2002. Homo on the range: Mobile and global sexualities. *Social Text* 20. (4) (Winter): 65–89.

Deshpande, Sundhanva. 2001. In the world of floating categories. *Himal Magazine*. 14 (6): 55–57.

Ebert, Roger. 1997. Fire strikes at Indian repression. *Chicago Sun Times*, September 7.

Filmfare. 1993. Clash: That's entertainment, that's politics. July.

Gandhi, Leela. 2002. Loving well: Homosexuality and utopian thought in post/colonial India. In *Queering India: Same-sex love and eroticism in Indian culture and society*, eds. Ruth Vanita and Saleem Kidwai. 88–89. New York: Routledge.

Gerstel, Judy. 1996. FilmFest '96. Canadians kick it off. *The Toronto Star*. September 6, 1996. http://www.thestar.com/editorial/filmfest/960906D01a_MO-MEHTA06.html.

Ghosh, Shohini. 1999a. Breaking the silences. *The Book Review*. XXIII (October):10.

———. 1999b. Troubled existence of sex and sexuality: Feminists engage with censorship. In *Image journeys: Audio-Visual media and cultural change in India*, eds. Christiane Brosius and Melissa Butcher. 233–59. New Delhi: Sage Publications.

———. 1999c. From the frying pan into the *Fire*. Special report. *Communalism Combat*. (January): 16–19.

———. 2000. Queering the family: Sexual and textual preferences in Indian fiction. *The Little Magazine* (November–December): 38–45.

——— 2002. Queer pleasures for queer people: Film, television and queer sexuality in India. In *Queering India*, 207–33.

———. 2007. False appearances and mistaken identities: The phobic and the erotic in Bombay cinema's queer vision. In *The Phobic and the Erotic*: 417–436.

———. 2010. The wonderful world of queer cinephilia. *Bioscope: South Asian Screen Studies* 1(1): 17–20.

Gopinath, Gayatri. 1998. On fire. *GLQ: A Journal of Lesbian and Gay Studies* 4(4): 631–36.

———. 2005. *Impossible desires: queer diasporas and South Asian public cultures*. Durham: Duke University Press.

The Hindu. 1998. Fire goes up in smoke. December 13.

Hindustan Times. 1998. Lead editorial. February 26.

Hindustan Times. 1998. Shiv Sainiks strip to tease Dilip Kuman over *Fire*. December 13.

Interviews and conversations: Deepa Mehta. 2003. *Talk Cinema*. September 21. http://www.talkcinema.com, as cited on http://www. collectionscanada.gc.ca/women/030001-1258-e.html.

Jain, Jasbir. 2007. The diasporic eye and the evolving I: Deepa Mehta's Elements trilogy. In *Films, literature and culture: Deepa Mehta's Elements Trilogy*, ed. Jasbir Jain. 54–74. Jaipur: Rawat Publications.

John, Mary E. and Tejaswini Niranjana. 1999. Mirror politics: Fire, hindutva and Indian culture. *Economic and Political Weekly* (March 6–13): 581–84.

Johnson, Brian D. 1997. Forbidden flames. *Maclean's*. September 29:86.

Kamani, Ginu. 1997. Burning bright: A conversation with Deepa Mehta about *Fire*. *Trikone* (October):11–12.

Kapur, Anuradha. 1993. Deity to crusader: The changing iconography of Ram. In *Hindus and Others*, ed. Gyanendra Pandey, New Delhi: Viking Penguin.

Kapur, Ratna. 1999. Cultural politics of *Fire*. *Economic and Political Weekly* (May 22): 1297–1300.

———. 2005. *Erotic justice: Law and the new politics of postcolonialism*. New Delhi: Permanent Black.

Kamani, Ginu. 1997. Burning bright: A conversation with Deepa Mehta about *Fire*. *Trikone*, (October): 11–13.

Kishwar, Madhu. 1998. Naïve outpourings of a self-hating Indian: Deepa Mehta's *Fire*. *Manushi* 109 (November–December): 3–14.

Lacey, Liam. 1997. East meets West in Deepa Mehta. *The Globe and Mail* (Eastern Edition). September 20.

Lak, Daniel. 1998. Lesbian film sets India on fire. BBC News, November 13. http://news.bbc.co.uk/2/hi/south_asia/213417.stm

Levitin, Jacqueline. 2002a. Deepa Mehta as a transnational filmmaker, or you can't go home again. In *North of Everything: English-Canadian Cinema since 1980*, eds. William Beard and Jerry White. 270–93. Edmonton: University of Alberta Press.

———. 2002b. An introduction to Deepa Mehta: Making films in Canada and India. In *Women Filmmakers: Refocusing*, eds. Jacqueline Levitin, Judith Plessis, and Valerie Raoul. 273–83. Vancouver: University of British Columbia Press.

Malkani, K.R. 1998. Liberalism: Can we handle it? *Sunday Times of India*. November 22.

Mandy, Marie. 2000. DVD. *Filming desire: A journey through women's cinema*. Brussels: SAGA Film; Paris: the factory, in co-production with ARTE and the RTBF.

Mehta, Deepa. 1996. Director's diary. *Fire* Press Kit (on file with author).

Menon, Nivedita, 2007. Outing heteronormativity: Nation, citizen, feminist disruptions. In *Sexualities: Issues in contemporary Indian feminism*, ed. Nivedita Menon. 3–51. New Delhi: Women Unlimited/ Kali for Women.

Naim, C.M. 1999. Dissent on *Fire*. *Economic and Political Weekly* (April 17–24): 955–957.

Patel, Geeta. On *Fire*. In *Queering India*, 222–33.

Paul Kumar, Sukrita. 2000. *Ismat: Her Life, Her Times*, New Delhi: Katha.

Pioneer. 1998. *Fire* pulled out of cinema halls. December 3.

Pioneer. 1998. Lifeline. December 3.

S.L. 1999. Fire! Fire! It's the lesbians!: A personal account. In *Lesbian emergence: A Citizen's report*, Campaign for Lesbian Rights (CALERI).

Saltzman, Devyani. 2006. *Shooting* Water*: A mother daughter journey and the making of a film*. Delhi: Penguin Books.

Sarkar, Tanika. 2001. Mrinal Onno Itihasher Shakkhor Adhunikatar Dui Ek Din. In *Dharmo, Sahityaor Rajniti*. [Mrinal as signature of another history. In *A few days of modernity: Religion and politics*]. Calcutta: Biplab Das Publishers.

Sengupta, Jayita. 2009. Gendered subject(s) in Deepa Mehta's *Fire* and *Water*. In *Films, literature and culture: Deepa Mehta's Elements trilogy*, ed. Jasbir Jain, 100–18.

Singh, Ruchira. 1995. Homosexuality and the bold art of selling jeans. *Asian Age* (May 26).

Sinha, Nikhil. 2000. Doordarshan, public service and the impact of globalization." In *Broadcasting reform in India*, eds. Munroe E. Price and Stefaan G. Verhulst., 22-40, New Delhi: Oxford University Press.

The Statesman. 1998. Much heat in Rajya Sabha over *Fire*. December 4.

Subramanyam, Chitra. 1998. Is it un-Indian? *Asian Age* (December 10).

Thadani, Giti. 1996. *Sakhiyani: Lesbian desire in ancient and modern India*. New York: Cassel.

Time Magazine.1996. Cannes in Canada. September 23.

Uniyal, B.N. 1998. Fringe cultures and /or mainstream? *The Observer* (December): 13–19.

Van Gelder, Lawrence. 1996. Both epic and feminist from India: Review of *Fire*. *New York Times*. October 2.

Vanita, Ruth and Saleem Kidwai. 2001. *Same-sex love in India: Readings from literature and history*. New York: St. Martin's Press.

Waugh, Thomas. 2001. Queer Bollywood? or "I'm the player, you're the naïve one": Patterns of sexual subversion in recent Indian cinema. In *Keyframes: Popular film and cultural studies*, eds. Matthew Tinkcom and Amy Villarejo. 280–98. New York: Routledge.

———. 2006. Deepa Mehta. In *The romance of transgression in Canada: Queering sexualities, nations, cinemas*. 468–69. Montreal: McGill-Queen's University Press.

White, Patricia.1999. *Uninvited: Classical Hollywood Cinema and Lesbian Representability.* Bloomington: Indiana University Press.

FILMOGRAPHY

Adhikar (*Rights*, TV), *Aur Shama Jalti ahin* (*And the Flame Kept Burning*), Lekh Tandon, Zee TV.

Anand (*Joy*), Hrishikesh Mukherjee, India, 1971, 122 min.

At 99: A Portrait of Louise Tandy Murch, Deepa Mehta, Canada, 1976, 24 min.

Ankur (*The Seedling*), Shyam Benegal, India, 1974, 131 min.

Anurodh (*Request*), Shakti Samanta, India, 1977, 147 min.

Arth (*Meaning*), Mahesh Bhatt, India, 1982, 138 min.

Bandit Queen, Shekhar Kapur, India, 1994, 119 min.

Bend It Like Beckham, Gurinder Chadha, UK, 2002, 112 min.

Bollywood/Hollywood, Deepa Mehta, Canada, 2002, 105 min.

BomGay, Riyad Wadia, India, 1996, 12 min.

Camilla, Deepa Mehta, Canada, 1994, 95 min.

The Crying Game, Neil Jordan, UK, 1992, 112 min.

Daayraa (*The Square Circle*), Amol Palekar, India, 1997, 107 min.

Danger Bay (TV), Deepa Mehta, Canada. Episodes: "This Little Piggy" (1989), "Ancient Spirits" (1990), "Hijacked" (1990), 30 min.

Darmiyaan: In Between, Kalpana Lazmi, India, 1997, 150 min.

Dilwale Dulhaniya Le Jayenge (*The Lover Gets the Bride*), Aditya Chopra, India, 1995, 189 min.

Dostana (*Friendship*), Tarun Mansukhani, India, 2008, 142 min.

Dosti (*Friendship*), Satyen Bose, India, 1964, 163 min.

Double the Trouble Twice the Fun, Pratibha Parmar, UK, 1992, 24 min.

Dulara (*The Loved One*), Vimal Kumar, India, 1993, 120 min.

Earth, Deepa Mehta, Canada, 1998, 110 min.

Electric Moon, Pradip Krishen, UK, 1992, 102 min.

Ek Baar Phir (*Once Again*), Vinod Pande, India, 1980, 157 min.

Filming Desire: A Journey through Women's Cinema, Marie Mandy, France, 2000, 60 min.

Fire, Deepa Mehta, Canada, 1996, 108 min.

Flesh and Paper, Pratibha Parmar, UK, 1990, 26 min.

Girlfriend, Karan Razdan, India, 2004, 125 min.

Hasratein (*Desires*, TV), Ajai Sinha, India.

Heaven on Earth, Deepa Mehta, Canada, 2008, 106 min.

Humjoli (*Beloved Friend*), Ramanna, India, 1970, 102 min.

Jodie, Pratibha Parmar, UK, 1996, 25 min.

Kal Ho Naa Ho (*If Tomorrow Never Comes*), Nikhil Advani, India, 2003, 186 min.

Kabhi Kabhi (*Once in a While*, TV), Mahesh Bhatt, Star Plus.

Khalnayak (*The Villain*), Subhash Ghai, India, 1993, 190 min.

Khuddar (*Man of Integrity*), Iqbal Durrani, India, 1993, 150 min.

Khush (*Happy*), Pratibha Parmar, UK, 1991, 26 min.

Let's Talk About It, Deepa Mehta, Canada, 2006, 47 min.

Main Khiladi Tu Anari (*I Am the Expert and You're Amateur*), Sameer Malkan, India, 1994, 175 min.

Mandi (*Marketplace*), Shyam Benegal, India, 1983, 167 min.

Martha, Ruth and Edie, Deepa Mehta, Canada, 1988, 92 min.

Masti (*Pranks*), Indra Kumar, India, 2004, 166 min.

Men Not Allowed, Shrey Srivastava, India, 2006, 96 min.

Mujhe Chand Chahiye (*I Want the Moon*, TV), Raja Bundela, Zee TV.

My Brother Nikhil, Onir, India, 2005, 120 min.

Mere Mehboob (*My Beloved*), Harnam Singh Rawail, India, 1963, 164 min.

A Mermaid Called Aida, Riyad Wadia, India, 1996, 52 min.

Naam (*Name*), Mahesh Bhatt, India, 1986, 120 min.

Namak Haram (*The Traitor*), Hrishikesh Mukherjee, India, 1973, 146 min.

Nina's Heavenly Delights, Pratibha Parmar, UK, 2006, 94 min.

A Place of Rage, Pratibha Parmar, USA, 1991, 54 min.

Razia Sultan (*Queen Razia*), Kamal Amrohi, India, 1983, 176 min.

The Republic of Love, Deepa Mehta, Canada, 2004, 95 min.

Sam and Me, Deepa Mehta, Canada, 1991, 94 min.

Sangam (*Confluence*), Raj Kapoor, India, 1964, 238 min.

Sari Red, Pratibha Parmar, UK, 1988, 11 min.

Shabnam Mausi (*Shabnam Aunty*), Yogesh Bhardwaj, India, 2005, 91 min.

Sholay (*Embers*), Ramesh Sippy, India, 1975, 188 min.

Streer Patra (*Letter from the Wife*), Purnendu Pattrea, India, 1976, 151 min.

Summer in My Veins, Nishit Saran, India, 1998, 41 min.

Tamanna (*Longing*), Mahesh Bhatt, India, 1997, 150 min.

Ushno Taar Jonno (*Warm for Her/For the Sake of Warmth*, TV), Kaushik
    Ganguly, India, 2002.

Water, Deepa Mehta, Canada, 2005, 114 min.

Yaraana (*Friendship*), Rakesh Kumar, India, 1981, 138 min.

Y*eh Aag Kab Bujhegi* (*When Will This Fire Be Doused?*), Sunil Dutt, India,
    1991, 150 min.

The Young Indiana Jones Chronicles (TV), Deepa Mehta, USA, 1993.
    Episodes: "Benares" (1993); "Greece," (1996).

Zakhm (*The Wound*), Mahesh Bhatt, India, 1998, 123 min.

INDEX

Note: Page numbers for photographs in **bold**. Film character names in quotation marks and not inverted, e.g., "Sita," "Radha."

SHOHINI GHOSH is Professor at the AJK Mass Communication Research Centre, Jamia Millia Islamia, a university in New Delhi. *Tales of the Night Fairies*, her documentary on the sex workers' rights movement, made a strong intervention in debates on sex work. She writes on contemporary media practices and sexuality.

About the editors

MATTHEW HAYS is a Montreal-based critic, author, programmer and university instructor. He has been a film critic and reporter for the weekly *Montreal Mirror* since 1993. His first book, *The View from Here: Conversations with Gay and Lesbian Filmmakers* (Arsenal Pulp Press), won a 2008 Lambda Literary Award. His articles have appeared in a broad range of publications, including *The Guardian*, *The Daily Beast*, *The Globe and Mail*, *The New York Times*, CBC Arts Online, *The Walrus*, *The Advocate*, *The Toronto Star*, *The International Herald Tribune*, *Cineaste*, *Cineaction*, *The Hollywood Reporter*, *Canadian Screenwriter*, *Xtra* and *fab*. He teaches courses in journalism, communication studies, and film studies at Concordia University, where he received his MA in communication studies in 2000.

THOMAS WAUGH is the award-winning author of numerous books, including five for Arsenal Pulp Press: *Out/Lines*, *Lust Unearthed*, *Gay Art: A Historic Collection* (with Felix Lance Falkon), *Comin' at Ya!* (with David Chapman), and *Montreal Main: A Queer Film Classic* (with Jason Garrison). His other books include *Hard to Imagine*, *The Fruit Machine*, and *The Romance of Transgression in Canada*. He teaches film studies at Concordia University in Montreal, Canada, where he lives. He has taught and published widely on political discourses and sexual representation in film and video, on queer film and video, and has developed interdisciplinary research and teaching on AIDS. He is also the founder and coordinator of the program in Interdisciplinary Studies in Sexuality at Concordia.

Titles in the Queer Film Classics series: